Business Result

SECOND EDITION

Elementary *Student's Book* with Online practice

OXFORD
UNIVERSITY PRESS

David Grant, John Hughes,
Nina Leeke & Rebecca Turner

Contents

Introduction

What's in a unit?

Starting point
- an introduction to the theme of the unit
- discussion questions

Working with words
- reading and listening about a work-related topic
- focus on key words and phrases
- practise the new words in speaking activities

Language at work
- grammar presented in authentic work contexts
- *Language point* box focuses on the key grammar points
- practise using the language in real work situations

Practically speaking
- focus on an aspect of everyday communication at work
- helps you to sound more natural when speaking
- practise speaking in real work situations

Business communication
- key expressions for authentic work contexts
- improve your communication skills for meetings, presentations, socializing, and phone calls
- *Key expressions* list in every unit

Talking point
- focus on interesting business topics and concepts
- improve your fluency with *Discussion* and *Task* activities
- *Discussion* and *Task* allow you to apply the topic to your own area of work

What's in the *Communication activities*?

- roles and information for pair and group activities
- extra speaking practice for the main sections of each unit

What's in the *Viewpoint* lessons?

The *Viewpoints* are video lessons, which appear after every three units. The topics of the *Viewpoint* lessons relate to a theme from the main units and include:
- interviews with expert speakers
- case studies of real companies

Each *Viewpoint* is divided into three or four sections, with a number of short video clips in each lesson. A *Viewpoint* lesson usually includes:
- A focus to introduce the topic. This contains a short video showing people discussing the topic.
- Key vocabulary and phrases which appear in the videos.
- Main video sections which develop listening and note-taking skills, and build confidence in listening to authentic language in an authentic context.
- Activities which provide speaking practice about the topic of the lesson.

All of the videos in the *Viewpoint* lessons can be streamed or downloaded from the *Online practice*.

What's in the *Practice files*?

Written exercises to practise the key language in:
- *Working with words*
- *Business communication*
- *Language at work*

Use the *Practice files*:
- in class to check your understanding
- out of class for extra practice or homework

The *Practice files* include a *Grammar reference* section with more detailed explanations of the grammar from each unit.

Follow the links (as shown below) to the *Practice file* in each unit.

>> For more exercises, go to **Practice file 6** on page 96

>> For more information, go to **Grammar reference** on page 97

What's in the *Online practice*?

- practice exercises for each *Working with words, Language at work* and *Business communication* section
- unit tests
- email exercises for each unit
- automatic marking for instant answers
- gradebook to check your scores and progress

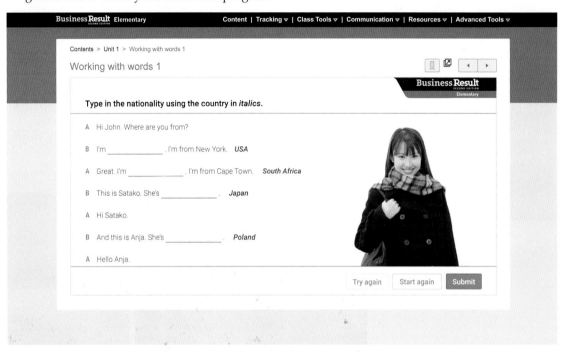

Additional resources

- watch and download all of the *Viewpoint* videos
- listen to and download all of the class audio
- sample emails for each unit

How to access your *Online practice*

To access your *Online practice*, you will find an access card on the inside cover of your Student's Book. This contains an access code to unlock all the content in the *Online practice*.

Go to **www.oxfordlearn.com** and activate your code, and then follow the instructions online to access the content.

1 Jobs

Starting point

1 What is your name?

2 What is the name of your company?

3 What is your job?

Working with words | Countries, nationalities, jobs

1 Look at these people. Say where they are from using words from the list.

Example: *Dahlia is from India.*

India   the UK   Japan   Poland   Brazil   the USA   Italy   South Africa

Dahlia

Raquel

Randy

Lukasz

Tiziana

Charlotte

Yuko

Jacob

2 ▶ 1.1 Say the nationality of the people using words from the list. Then listen and check.

> *Example: Dahlia is Indian.*

Indian   British   Japanese   Polish   Brazilian
American   Italian   South African

3 ▶ 1.2 Listen and <u>underline</u> the stress on these words.

Japan   Japanese   British   Italy   Italian
India   American   Brazilian   Polish   Africa

4 ▶ 1.3 Look at the people in **1** again. Listen and write their job titles in the table. Use the words from the list.

Sales Rep   Financial Director   Chief Executive Officer   Personal Assistant
Technician   Human Resources Manager   ~~Receptionist~~   Team Leader

	Name	Job title	Nationality of company
1	Dahlia	*Receptionist*	
2	Raquel		
3	Randy		
4	Lukasz		
5	Tiziana		
6	Charlotte		
7	Yuko		
8	Jacob		

5 ▶ 1.3 Listen again and write the nationality of the speakers' companies in the table in **4**.

6 Which jobs in **4** are in your company? Which other jobs are in your company?

7 Work with a partner. Think of other directors, assistants and managers.

<u>*marketing*</u> director   <u>*sales*</u> assistant   <u>*technical*</u> manager

_____   _____   _____

_____   _____   _____

>> For more exercises, go to **Practice file 1** on page 86.

8 Complete this information about yourself.

My country: _____
My nationality: _____
My job: _____
Nationality of my company: _____

9 Work with a partner. Tell him/her about the information in **8**.

I'm from …
I'm …
I'm a/an …
My company is …

10 Now tell the class about your partner.

He's/She's from …
He's/She's …
He's/She's a/an …
His/Her company is …

Tip | a/an

Use *a/an* before a job or company:
*I'm **a** receptionist with **an** American company.*
Use *an* before a vowel sound:
***an** American, **an** Italian.*

Language at work | Present simple | Possessives

1 Read about the company Marcegaglia and complete the profile.

Company name: ___*Marcegaglia*___   Head office: _____

Products: _____   CEO: _____

MARCEGAGLIA

Marcegaglia **is** an Italian company and one of its main products **is** steel pipes. The company's head office **is** in Italy, near Milan, but its customers **aren't** only Italian. They **are** in countries all over the world. Marcegaglia **is** a family company. Antonio Marcegaglia and his sister Emma **are** the Chief Executive Officers. For Emma, the family company **isn't** her only job. She **is** also the leader of the oil and gas company Eni.

2 Complete the table in *Language point 1* below. Use the words in **bold** from the text in **1**.

LANGUAGE POINT 1

	Positive	Negative	Questions	Short answers
I	___*am*___ …	___*am not*___ …	Am I …?	Yes, I am.
		(___*'m not*___ …)		No, I'm not.
You/We/They	_____ …	_____ …	Are you/we/they …?	Yes, you/we/they are.
		(_____ …)		No, you/we/they aren't.
He/She/It	_____ …	_____ …	Is he/she/it …?	Yes, he/she/it is.
		(_____ …)		No, he/she/it isn't.

>> For more information, go to **Grammar reference** on page 87.

3 ▶1.4 Read the interview about Marcegaglia. <u>Underline</u> the correct verbs in *italics*. Then listen and check.

A So, ¹*is / are* Marcegaglia a family company?

B Yes, it ²*is / am*. Steno Marcegaglia started the company in 1959, and his children Antonio and Emma ³*is / are* the CEOs.

A ⁴*Is / Are* they from a big family?

B No, they ⁵*'s / 're* from a small family, but Marcegaglia ⁶*isn't / 'm not* a small company. It ⁷*'s / 're* a multi-billion euro company with 7,000 employees.

A And ⁸*is / are* all the employees in Italy?

B They ⁹*is / are* in Italy and in many other countries, too, such as Brazil and China.

4 Complete sentences 1–5 with the correct form of the verb *be*. Make the sentence true about you.

Example: I'm not Spanish. (I'm French.)

1 I'_____ Spanish.

2 My company _____ Polish.

3 Our customers _____ in Asia.

4 My work colleagues _____ my friends.

5 English _____ important in my company/job.

Tip | *'m or am?*

We use *'m*, *'s* or *'re* for speaking or for informal writing (e.g. emails to colleagues):

I'm = I am

She's = She is

They're = They are

We use *am*, *is* or *are* for short answers:

Are you at work all the time?

Yes, I am. NOT *Yes, I'm.*

Tip | *it's or its?*

It is = It's:
My company is Toyota. **It's** a car company.

Its = possessive:
My company is Toyota. **Its** CEO is Akio Toyoda.

5 Read the possessive sentences in *Language point 2*. Use the words in **bold** to complete the table.

LANGUAGE POINT 2

Is **your** company American?
My company is Italian.
Our company is a steel company.
Its customers are all over the world.
Emma is CEO. **Her** brother Antonio is also CEO.
Their father started the company. **His** name was Steno.

I → ___my___	you → _____	he → _____	she → _____
	it → _____	we → _____	they → _____

6 Work with a partner. Look again at the sentences in **4**. Ask and answer questions about the sentences with Is/Are …?
   Example: **A** Are you Spanish?   **B** Yes, I am. / No, I'm not.

7 Look at the profile of Sofia Aguilera. Complete the interview with her below. Use words from **5**.

Name: Sofia Aguilera
Country: Mexico
Company name: Webmex Solutions
Job: Managing Director
Customers: Small businesses

Interviewer Is ¹ ___your___ business a family company?
Sofia Yes, it is. ²_____ husband is the Technical Manager. ³_____ name is Orial. And ⁴_____ daughter is the Sales Manager. ⁵_____ name is Martina.
Interviewer Is it an IT company?
Sofia Yes, it is. ⁶_____ customers are small businesses. We work with ⁷_____ websites.

>> For more exercises, go to **Practice file 1** on page 87.

8 Work with a partner. Look at some profiles on a website. **Student A**, turn to **page 110**. **Student B**, turn to **page 115**.

9 Ask questions to find out about your partner's job. Use the information to write a company profile, similar to Marcegaglia in **1**.

Practically speaking | How to spell

1 ▶1.5 Listen and repeat the groups of letters. Why are they in these groups?
   1 A H J K   4 I Y   6 Q U W
   2 B C D E G P T V (Z) 5 O   7 R
   3 F L M N S X (Z)

2 ▶1.6 Listen to two conversations. Write the names.
   1 _____   2 _____

3 What is the question in each conversation? _____

4 Work with a partner. Say and spell:
   • your name   • your company's name   • your job title

Business communication | Saying hello and goodbye

1 ▶ 1.7 Two visitors are in Reception. Listen and complete this visitor board.

FRIDAY 12TH SEPTEMBER

WELCOME TODAY TO:
MR ALEK ¹_____
MS ²_____ WOZNIAK

VISITING:
MRS ³_____ DA ROCHA

2 ▶ 1.7 Match expressions 1–6 to responses a–f. Then listen and check.

1 Hello. My name is Alek Gorski. ___
2 I'm Eva, Maria Da Rocha's assistant. ___
3 This is my assistant, Elzbieta Wozniak. ___
4 It's good to see you again. ___
5 How are you? ___
6 Do you know Elzbieta? ___

a Pleased to meet you.
b No. How do you do?
c How do you do, Mr Gorski?
d I'm fine.
e Nice to meet you.
f And you.

3 Put expressions 1–6 and their responses in **2** into these categories.

1 Saying hello and introducing yourself: _1c_ , ___
2 Introducing someone: ___ , ___
3 Saying hello to someone you know: ___ , ___

4 Work in groups of three. Practise this conversation.

A Say hello to B (a colleague).

B Say hello to A (a colleague) and introduce C.

C Say hello to A (this is your first meeting).

5 Now change roles and practise the conversation again.

6 Complete this conversation with the expressions from the list.

Have a good journey   See you soon   Nice meeting you

Maria   ¹_____, Alek.
Alek   Yes, goodbye, Maria.
Maria   ²_____, Elzbieta.
Elzbieta   Nice meeting you, too.
Maria   Bye. ³_____.
Alek   Thanks. Bye.

7 ▶ 1.8 Listen and check. Then practise the conversation in **6** in your groups of three.

>> For more exercises, go to **Practice file 1** on page 86.

8 Repeat the conversation in **4** and then say goodbye to Student A, B or C.

Key expressions

Saying hello and introducing yourself
Hello. My name is ... / I'm ...
Pleased to meet you.
How do you do?
Nice to meet you (too).

Introducing someone
This is ...
Do you know ...?

Saying hello to someone you know
It's good to see you again.
How are you?

Saying goodbye
Nice meeting you.
See you soon.
Have a good journey.
Goodbye/Bye.

TALKING POINT

The introductions game

Play the introductions game with a partner.

Begin on START. Toss a coin.
Heads = move 1 square.
Tails = move 2 squares.
On a white square, follow the instruction.
On a blue square, respond.
The winner arrives on FINISH first.

16 FINISH	**15** Tell your partner about your colleagues – names, jobs, nationalities.	**14** Goodbye.	**13** Introduce your partner to a customer.
9 Ask your partner: name? job? nationality?	**10** Are you from Japan?	**11** Introduce the person on card A to your partner.	**12** Tell your partner about your boss – name, job, nationality.
8 Are you French?	**7** Spell your company's name.	**6** Hello, my name's Annie Da Silva.	**5** Introduce yourself with the information on card B.
1 START	**2** Introduce yourself – give your name, job and nationality.	**3** Ask how your partner is.	**4** How do you spell your name?

A

NAME **MR STANISLAV BEYER**
JOB **MARKETING ASSISTANT** | **WARSAW, POLAND**

B

NAME
Ms Lesley Johnson

JOB
Technical Engineer
Middlesex, UK

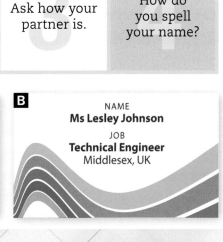

11

Starting point

1 What nationality are these companies: Lufthansa, Sony?

2 What do these companies produce: Philips, Bayer?

3 What do these companies provide: Banco do Brasil, CNN?

Working with words | Company types and activities

1 Match these company types to the pictures 1–8.

pharmaceuticals   real estate   electronics   recruitment
hotel   software   financial services   automobile

1 _____

2 _____

3 _____

4 _____

5 _____

6 _____

7 _____

8 _____

2 ▶ 2.1 Listen to three people at a job fair. Which words do you hear from 1?

3 ▶ 2.1 Listen again and complete these sentences.
1 Natasha works for a _____ company. She provides staff in the _____ industry.
2 Malik's company produces _____ for _____ companies.
3 William works in _____. He wants a job in the _____ industry.

4 ▶ 2.2 Listen and underline the stress in these words.

pharma<u>ceu</u>ticals   electronics   recruitment
hotel   finance   automobile

5 What type of company is your company? What type of companies do you work with?

6 A company produces products and it provides services. Write *product* or *service* next to the words in 1–6.

A	B	C
GlaxoSmithKline		electronic equipment ^{1} _product_
Microsoft		finance ^{2}_____
Sony	provides/produces	software ^{3}_____
Manpower		cars ^{4}_____
Toyota		staff ^{5}_____
Deutsche Bank AG		pharmaceuticals ^{6}_____

7 Work with a partner. Take turns to make sentences about the companies in **6**.
Example: Sony produces electronic equipment.

8 Does your company produce products or provide services? Or both?

9 ▶ 2.3 Listen to a presentation about Kikkoman. Number the presentation slides A–D in the order you hear them 1–4.

A ___

B ___

C ___

D ___

10 Complete the presentation with the verbs from the list.

employ   sell   export   provide   buy   develop

Kikkoman is a Japanese company and we ^{1}_____ 400 million litres of soy sauce every year. We ^{2}_____ around 6,000 people in total. We ^{3}_____ soy sauce all over the world, including Asia, North America, Australia and Europe. We also ^{4}_____ new products for the pharmaceuticals industry. Restaurants, supermarkets and Asian food shops ^{5}_____ our products and we also ^{6}_____ lessons in Japanese cooking – using Kikkoman products, of course!

11 ▶ 2.3 Listen again and check your answers to **10**.

≫ For more exercises, go to **Practice file 2** on page 88.

12 Prepare a presentation about your company. Use some of the sentences below.
1 I'm _____
2 I'm from _____
3 I work for _____
4 We produce/provide _____
5 We employ _____
6 We develop _____
7 We export to _____
8 We sell our products to _____

13 Now give your presentation to the class.

Tip | *work* + preposition
We use the verb *work* in different ways:
work **for** (an employer/company): I **work for** BMW.
work **with** (people or another country): I **work with** colleagues.
work **in** (department or area of business): I **work in** Production.

Language at work | Present simple

1 CJ is a Korean company with different business areas. Match these business areas to pictures A–D below.

Bio Pharma   *Home Shopping and Logistics*
Food and Food Service   *Entertainment and Media*

A _____

We ¹*produce / produces* sugar and cooking oil. The company ²*have / has* restaurants, cafés and food shops. It ³*provide / provides* meals for restaurants, schools and hospitals.

B _____

We ⁴*export / exports* medicines to countries around the world and we ⁵*develop / develops* new biotechnological products.

C _____

The company ⁶*produce / produces* films for the Korean market and abroad. We ⁷*import / imports* films from foreign production companies ... and we ⁸*have / has* eight cable TV channels ... and a chain of cinemas.

D _____

We ⁹*provide / provides* a home shopping service. We ¹⁰*have / has* a logistics centre. It ¹¹*provide / provides* transport and delivery services.

2 ▶ 2.4 Listen to an interview about CJ and underline the correct verbs in *italics* in **1**.

3 ▶ 2.5 Listen and complete these questions and answers about CJ.

1 **A** _____ _____ export these products?
   B Yes, we _____.
2 **A** _____ the _____ import films, too?
   B Yes, _____ _____.
3 **A** _____ CJ provide financial services?
   B No, it _____ provide financial services.
4 **A** _____ you _____ medicines?
   B No, _____ _____. We export medicines.

Tip | *have/has*
The verb *have* is irregular:
I **have** → *It* **has** NOT ~~It haves~~

4 Answer the questions in the *Language point*.

> **LANGUAGE POINT**
>
> The verbs in **1** are in the present simple. We use the present simple for general facts. Complete explanations 1–5 of how to form the present simple.
> 1 We add *-s* or *-es* to the verb after *he, she* and ___ .
> 2 We make questions with the words _____ and _____ .
> 3 We make negative sentences with the words _____ and _____ .
> 4 We make positive short answers with *Yes, he* _____ / *Yes, I* _____ .
> 5 We make negative short answers with *No, she* _____ / *No, we* _____ .
>
> In conversation, we answer questions with short answers.
>   **A** *Do you export these products?*
>   **B** *Yes, we do.* NOT ~~Yes, we export~~.

» For more information, go to **Grammar reference** on page 89.

5 Work with a partner. Name a company from a business area in **1**. Use the words in *italics* to talk about the company.
    Example: *Canal Plus is a media company. It produces films for the European market.*

6 Work with a partner. Ask and answer questions using the prompts below.
… you work for …?
… your company export / import …?
… your company produce / provide …?
… your company develop / deliver …?
… you have …?
… your department employ …?
… your customers buy …?
    Example: **A** *Do you work for an Italian company?*
                 B *No, I don't. I work for a Brazilian company.*

» For more exercises, go to **Practice file 2** on page 89.

Practically speaking | How to say numbers

1 Can you say the numbers in A–D?

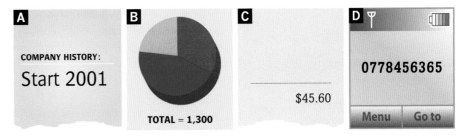

2 ▶ 2.6 Listen and match A–D in **1** to the speakers 1–4.
    1 ___   2 ___   3 ___   4 ___

3 Work with a partner. Ask and answer these questions with numbers.
1 What year is it now?
2 What year is the next Olympic Games?
3 What's your office phone number?
4 What's your company's reception phone number?
5 What's the number of employees in your company?
6 What's the price of your company's main product or service?
7 What's the price of your journey to work?

Tip | Saying '0'
We say *oh* or *zero* for 0.

Business communication | Making phone calls

1 ▶ 2.7 Listen to two phone calls. Choose the correct names or words in *italics* to complete the sentences.

1 The receptionist puts *Anna / Peter* through to *Anna / Peter*.
2 Anna *knows / doesn't know* Peter.
3 Anna is calling about *the bank / an email*.
4 Raymond Saddler calls *his office / a hotel*.
5 The receptionist *puts / doesn't put* Raymond through to another person.
6 Raymond is calling about *meeting rooms / hotel rooms*.

2 ▶ 2.7 Listen to the two phone calls again. Who says these expressions from the two phone calls? Tick (✓) the correct box.

	Caller	'Receiver'/ Receptionist	Caller and 'Receiver'
1 Good morning. TE Media.			
2 Good morning. This is Anna Lillis from OPT Bank.			
3 Is Peter Bawden there, please?			
4 Yes, I'll put you through.			
5 Hello, Peter Bawden speaking.			
6 Hi, Peter. It's Anna Lillis.			
7 I'm calling about …			
8 See you (soon).			
9 Hello. The Dubai Grand Hotel.			
10 How can I help you?			
11 Thanks for your help.			
12 You're welcome.			

3 Complete the two phone calls. Use the expressions in **2** to help you. Practise the phone calls with your partner. Use your own name and company name.

1
A Hello, Dubai Hire Cars. How _____ I _____ you?
B Hello. This is _____ from _____. I'm _____ _____ your prices …
… and you can pay by credit card.
A That's great. Thanks for your _____.
B _____ welcome.
A Goodbye.
B _____.

2
A Good morning. _____
B Good morning. This is _____ from _____. _____ Niki Alstom _____, please?
A Yes, I'll _____ you _____.
B Thanks …
… Good. See you tomorrow then.
A Yes. _____ _____ _____. Bye.

>> For more exercises, go to **Practice file 2** on page 88.

4 Work in groups of two or three. Practise starting and ending phone calls. Use these reasons for calling, or your own ideas:
• today's meeting • next week's visit • the conference hotel

Hungary: country profile

Hungary is a European country and it exports many of its products to other European countries. Important products are cars, textiles and pharmaceuticals. Audi and Suzuki have factories in Hungary and export many cars. Hungary also produces wheat and sunflower seeds. It imports products from Europe, Russia and China. Oil and gas are very important imports. Many people visit Hungary, and hotels, restaurants and tourist companies provide services for them.

Discussion

1 What does Hungary export and import? What types of business are important in Hungary? Read the country profile and check your ideas.

2 Work with a partner or in small groups. Discuss these questions.
1 How is Hungary the same or different from your country?
2 What types of business are important in your country?
3 What does your country produce?
4 What products does it export and import?
5 What services does it provide?

Task

1 Work in groups of four. **Student A,** turn to **page 110. Student B,** turn to **page 116. Student C,** turn to **page 117. Student D,** turn to **page 114.** Take turns to read out each of your sentences. Use the information to complete your company profile.

3 Location

Starting point

1 Does your company have offices or operations in different countries? Where?

2 Do you always work in the same place? What places do you visit for your job?

3 Where is your head office?

Working with words | Location and workplace

1 Match the workplaces to pictures 1–5.

Research and development (R&D) centre   Factory
Distribution centre   Sales office   Head office

1 _____

2 _____

3 _____

4 _____

5 _____

2 Work with a partner. Read sentences 1–5. Which workplace from 1 do they describe?

1 We make all our products here.
2 We design new products here.
3 Our sales reps visit customers four days a week, but come here on Fridays.
4 The Managing Director and all the other company directors work here.
5 The products come here and we deliver them to customers.

3 Read about the LEGO Group. Where does it operate?

CHILD'S PLAY

LEGO® produces play materials for children. LEGO bricks and toys are popular all over the world and the company sells them in more than 140 countries. LEGO is a Danish company and its name is from the Danish phrase 'leg godt' (play well). It operates on six continents and has about 14,000 employees. There are also LEGOLAND® parks in Asia, Europe and North America.

4 Look at the map of LEGO's locations around the world. Match the continents below to the numbers from the map 1–6.

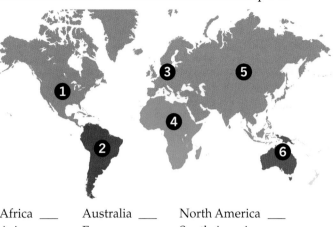

Africa ___   Australia ___   North America ___
Asia ___   Europe ___   South America ___

5 ▶ 3.1 Listen to a presentation about the LEGO group. How many sales offices are there in each continent? Write the numbers in the table.

Number of sales offices			
Europe		South America	
Asia		Australia	
North America		Africa	

6 ▶ 3.1 Listen to the presentation again. Tick (✓) the workplaces that are in each country in the table.

	Head office	R&D centre	Factory	Distribution centre
China				
Czech Republic				
Denmark				
Hungary				
Mexico				
USA				

» For more exercises, go to **Practice file 3** on page 90.

7 Prepare a presentation about your company or a company you know well, or use the information about the company below. Write notes about its workplaces and the locations. Give your presentation to your partner or the class. Use some of these phrases and audio script 3.1 to help you.
Good morning. Today, I'd like to tell you about …   We are … / We have …

Company:	AstraZeneca pharmaceuticals
Head office:	London, UK
R&D centres:	Södertälje, Sweden (+ in North America and India)
Factories:	27 in 19 countries
Sales offices:	32 in Europe
	16 in North America
	12 in South America
	28 in Asia and the Middle East
	13 in Africa and Australia

Language at work | *There is/are* | *Some/any*

1 Read about Singapore. Why is it a good location for business?

Three reasons to choose Singapore for your business

Location

Singapore is a small island country in the centre of South-East Asia, and it is the perfect place to do business in the region. **There are** flights to about 300 cities around the world from its busy Changi Airport, and **there is** a harbour for the import and export of goods by sea.

Business

Thousands of international businesses choose Singapore for their regional headquarters. **There are** low taxes for businesses to pay and **there aren't** any problems with visas for foreign workers. Singapore is also a great place to have a conference because **there are** hundreds of hotels and large exhibition centres. For example, **there is** the Changi Exhibition Centre near the airport.

The city

Singapore is a great place to live and work. **There are** some excellent schools, hospitals and other public services. And **there isn't** a crime problem – it's a very safe city.

2 Answer the questions in the *Language point*.

LANGUAGE POINT

Look at the words in **bold** in the text in **1**. Complete the table with *is*, *are*, *isn't* and *aren't*.

	Positive	Negative	Questions	Short answers
Singular noun:	There _____ (an airport).	There _____ (an airport).	_____ there (an airport)?	Yes, there _____. No, there _____.
Plural noun:	There _____ (two airports).	There _____ (two airports).	_____ there (two airports)?	Yes, there _____. No, there _____.

Read these sentences from the text in **1**. Choose the correct words in *italics* to complete the explanations 1–3.

> *There are **some** excellent schools, hospitals and other public services.*
> *There aren't **any** problems with visas for foreign workers.*

1 We use *some* and *any* with *singular / plural* nouns.
2 We use *some / any* with *there* in positive sentences.
3 We use *some / any* with *there* in negative sentences.

》 For more information, go to **Grammar reference** on page 91.

3 ▶ 3.2 Two people are discussing a location for a conference. Complete their conversation with the words from the list. Then listen and check.

there are   there is   there isn't   is there   are there

A Dubai is a great location for a conference. The weather is always good.
B What about the airport? [1]_____ lots of international flights?
A Yes, [2]_____. And [3]_____ a problem with transport from the airport because public transport is excellent in Dubai.
B But [4]_____ a good place for a conference?
A Yes, [5]_____. It's the Dubai International Exhibition and Convention complex. It's perfect.

》 For more exercises, go to **Practice file 3** on page 91.

4 Work with a partner. Ask and answer questions about two hotels in Dubai. **Student A**, turn to **page 116**. **Student B**, ask Student A about The Arabian Garden Hotel. Write notes in the table below.

Example: Is there a bus to the airport?

	The Arabian Garden Hotel	The Dubai Grand Hotel
Bus to the airport?		
Car park?		
Restaurants and bars?		
Leisure facilities (swimming pool, gym)?		
Services (Internet, bank)?		
Conference/Meeting rooms?		
Other services?		

5 Now repeat the exercise in **4**. **Student A**, ask Student B about The Dubai Grand Hotel and write notes in the table. **Student B**, turn to **page 116**.

6 Now compare the two hotels and choose one for a conference.

Practically speaking | Saying email and postal addresses

1 How do you say these email and postal addresses?
1 peter.tieng@forresters.ca
2 alina_dl@gmail.com
3 jobs-info@topcommunications.co.uk
4 Accounts Dept, Blair & Browns, 99 Edward Street, Toronto, M5V 2MD
5 21 Old School Rd, Glasgow, G21 4YU
6 742 Quaker St, Seattle, 98104

▶ 3.3 Listen and check. Practise the addresses with a partner.

2 Match symbols and abbreviations 1–8 to meanings a–h.

1 @ ___	5 St ___	a Street	e department
2 & ___	6 Rd ___	b Road	f hyphen (dash)
3 . ___	7 Dept ___	c at	g underscore
4 _ ___	8 - ___	d and	h dot

3 ▶ 3.4 Listen to a phone conversation. Complete the postal and email addresses.
Postal address: _____ _____ _____ , *Cambridge* , _____
Email address: *chris* _____

4 ▶ 3.4 Listen again. Number expressions a–i in the order you hear them 1–9.
a Can you spell … for me? ___
b What's the postcode, please? ___
c Sorry, can you repeat that, please? ___
d Can you give me your address, please? _1_
e Yes, that's right. ___
f What's your email address, please? ___
g Is that 30 …? ___
h No, it's … , not … ___
i So that's … ___

5 Work with a partner. Ask for and give contact details. **Student A**, turn to **page 110**. **Student B**, turn to **page 116**.

Tip | *all one word*
We don't have a space between two different words in email addresses:
*info@**fastshop**.com = info at fast shop, **all one word**, dot com*

Tip | British and American addresses
British and American English use different words in addresses:
postcode (British English) = *zip code* (American English)
postal address (British English) = *mailing address* (American English)

Business communication | Ordering by phone

1 Work with a partner. Discuss these questions.
1 Do you order products and services by phone? What do you order?
2 Do your customers order products and services by phone? What do they order?
3 Who are your suppliers at work? Where do they deliver their products?

2 ▶ 3.5 A customer calls a supplier. Listen to their conversation. Who asks for or about the things 1–7? Write *C* (customer) or *S* (supplier).
1 three whiteboards ___
2 the product code ___
3 the price ___
4 to deliver tomorrow ___
5 a delivery address ___
6 to confirm by email ___
7 an email address ___

3 ▶ 3.5 Listen again and complete these questions with the words from the list.

I (x3)   you (x4)   me   ~~order~~   repeat   tell   confirm   say   have   check

1 Can ____*I*____ ___*order*___ some whiteboards, please?
2 Can _____ _____ _____ the product code?
3 Can _____ _____ the delivery time, please?
4 Can _____ _____ your delivery address?
5 Can _____ _____ the post code, please?
6 Can _____ _____ my order by email, please?
7 Can _____ _____ that more slowly?

4 ▶ 3.5 Listen to the conversation again. Complete the table with these expressions.

Got it.   I'm sorry, but …   Sure.   Yes, of course.   Yes, that's right.

Saying 'yes' to a request	Saying 'no' to a request	Saying you understand	Saying something is correct

5 Work with a partner. Take turns to ask and answer the questions in **3**.

》 For more exercises, go to **Practice file 3** on page 90.

6 Work with a partner. Student A, call Student B to order some mobile phones. Use the prompts below to have a conversation.

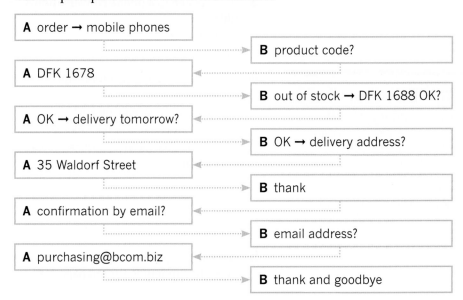

7 Work with a partner. Practise ordering by phone. **Student A**, turn to **page 110. Student B**, turn to **page 116.**

Key expressions

Asking to do something
Can I order …?

Asking for information
Can you tell me …?
Can you confirm …?
Can I have …?
Can I check …?

Asking for repetition
Can you repeat that?
Can you say that again?
Can you say that more slowly, please?

Responding
Yes, of course.
Sure.
(Yes) That's right.
I'm sorry, but …
Got it.
OK (thanks).

TALKING POINT

What is the best city for your conference?

Before you choose the right hotel or conference centre for your event, it is important to choose the best city. How do you choose the best city? These questions can help you:

- Is it easy for people to arrive in the city by air, train or car? People don't want to have a difficult journey to get to your event.
- Is it easy to travel around the city after you arrive? For example, from the airport to the city or from the train station to the conference location. Is there a good public transport system or taxi service?

- Is there a good choice of conference centres and hotels? Do these places have good facilities? For example, car parking space, restaurants, meeting rooms, Internet access.
- How much does it cost? Is transport and accommodation in the city cheap, or expensive?

The answers to these questions can help you find the perfect city for your conference.

Discussion

1   How do you choose the best city for a conference? Read the article above for some ideas. Can you think of any other ideas?

2   Do you go to conferences? What is good or bad about the conference locations?

3   Is your city a good location for a conference? Why/Why not?

4   What do you think is the perfect location for a conference? Why?

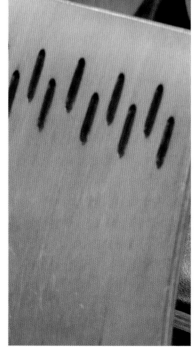

Task

1   Work with a partner. Read about two different cities: Vienna and Vancouver. **Student A**, turn to **page 111**. **Student B**, turn to **page 117**.

2   Take turns to tell your partner about each city. While you listen to your partner, complete your table with details about the other city.

3   Which city do you think is the best for an international conference, using the ideas from the article above?

Focus

1 Work with a partner. Practise this conversation.
Student A: You are in your place of work. Welcome a new visitor and talk about your workplace.
Student B: You are the visitor. Ask Student A questions about his/her job, company and place of work.

2 Swap roles in 1 and repeat the conversation.

3 ▶01 Watch five people talking about their job, company and place of work. Make notes about their answers in the table.

	Job	Company	Place of work
Speaker 1			
Speaker 2			
Speaker 3			
Speaker 4			
Speaker 5			

4 Compare your notes in 3 with a partner.

Describing an office

5 Read these groups of words for describing an office. Which word is NOT correct in each group?
1 Furniture: desk, shelves, webcam, chair
2 Equipment: phone, printer, door, laptop
3 Age: modern, new, quiet, old
4 Facilities: kitchen, client, toilets, parking
5 Size: noisy, small, big, medium-sized
6 Appearance: fast, attractive, beautiful, light

6 ▶02 Watch a video of different offices. Which words in **5** describe what you see?

7 Work with a partner. Describe your office or place of work using the words in **5**.

Example: It has three desks with phones. It's modern and there are good facilities.

Looking at offices

8 ▶03 Tom Sutherland is a web designer. At the moment he works from home but he needs an office. Watch Part 1 of the video and answer questions 1–3.
  1 Why does Tom want a new office?
  2 Where is the first office?
  3 What equipment and facilities are there in the first office?

9 ▶04 Now watch Part 2 of the video and answer questions 1–3.
  1 Where is the second office?
  2 What equipment and facilities are there in the second office?
  3 Can Tom decide?

10 ▶05 Watch the whole video again. Write down positive and negative things about each office.

	Positive	Negative
Office 1		
Office 2		

Choosing an office

11 Work with a partner. Which is the best office for Tom? Discuss these things:
  • the location and facilities
  • the furniture and equipment
  • the age, size and appearance

12 Present your answers in **11** to the class. Do you all agree? Why/Why not?

4 Technology

Starting point

1 What technology do you use for work?

2 Do you use the same technology at home?

3 Compare your answers with the class.

Working with words | Technology and functions

1 Do you use online or mobile banking? Why/Why not?

2 Read this text about mobile banking. Why is mobile banking useful?

MONEY ON THE MOVE

*All over the world more and more people use mobile banking. In the UK, experts say that 60% of adults will use their smartphone or **tablet** to manage their money by the year 2020.*

To start, just **download** your bank's mobile banking **app** onto your smartphone or tablet and register your mobile device. If you don't want to download the app, you can access the bank's website on your tablet or laptop.

With some banks in the UK, you can use the *Paym* payment system to send and receive money to and from your friends and family. You don't need their bank account information, only their mobile phone number.

With mobile banking, you can:
- **Log in** and access your **bank account** anytime you have **Internet access**.
- See all your accounts and move money easily between accounts.

3 Match the words in **bold** from the text in **2** to pictures 1–6.

    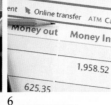

1 _____ 2 _____ 3 _____ 4 _____ 5 _____ 6 _____

4 ▶ 4.1 Listen to the conversation about the *Paym* system. Number the stages a–e in the correct order 1–5.

a ___ log in to your mobile banking

b ___ register for the *Paym* service

c ___ the person who gets the money receives an SMS message confirmation of the payment

d ___ open your mobile banking app or the bank's website

e ___ enter the details, for example the amount of money you want to send

5 ▶ 4.2 Work with a partner. Use the words from the list to complete these phrases from the conversation. Then listen and check.

text message   contact list   battery   username   screen   button
password   power point   link

1   Log in (to your account) with your _____ and _____.
2   Press the *Paym* _____ or click on the *Paym* _____ if you are using your laptop.
3   On the next _____ you can enter the details.
4   It's a bit like sending a _____.
5   Select someone from your _____.
6   A I need to charge my phone first. The _____ is low.
    B OK. There's a _____ over here.

6   Match the verbs in A to the nouns in B.

A	B
access	a battery / a phone
charge/recharge	a button / a link
click on	a contact / an account
download	a device / for a service
key in / enter	a text message / money
link	a website / an account
log in (to) / log out (of)	an account / a device
register	an account / a website
select	an app
send/receive	the details / a phone number

≫ For more exercises, go to **Practice file 4** on page 92.

7   Look at actions 1–6. Make verb + noun phrases about each picture.

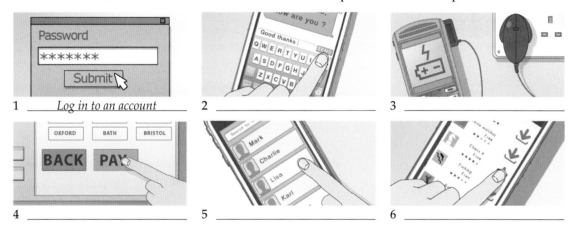

1   *Log in to an account*
2   _____
3   _____
4   _____
5   _____
6   _____

Tip | *sign in/out/up*

sign in/out = log in/out:
Are you a flighttickets.com customer? **Sign in** here
sign up = register for a service for the first time:
Are you a new customer? **Sign up** here

8   Work with a partner. Tick (✓) the actions in **6** and **7** that you do at work. Tell your partner when you do the actions.

> ***Example:*** *I log in to my email account every morning. I recharge my phone battery once a week.*

9   Technology words are often the same or similar in different languages. Are the words in **5** and **6** similar in your language? What about other technology words?

Language at work | Adverbs of frequency | Questions

1 Do you work eight hours a day? How many hours a week do you work?

2 Read this article and answer questions 1–3.
1 Do they work eight hours a day?
2 Do they arrive on time?
3 Do they take breaks?

THE SUPER EMPLOYEES!

How often do you work nine or ten hours a day? Well, imagine these workers: They **always** work 16 hours a day, seven days a week. They are never late for work because they **never** leave the building. They **rarely** take breaks – only to recharge their batteries. Of course, they aren't human, they're robots.

So where do these robots work? Staples – the US office product distributor – employs them in its warehouse in Chambersburg, Pennsylvania. 50% of staff are robots who move items around the warehouse. Because the new 'employees' are so good, Staples wants more in its other 29 warehouses.

3 Does your company use robots? If not, do you have jobs for a robot in your place of work?

4 Answer the questions in *Language point 1*.

LANGUAGE POINT 1

Complete this scale with the adverbs in **bold** in **2**.

| 1 _____ | 2 _____ | *sometimes* | *often* | *usually* | 3 _____ |

0% •————————————— 50% ————————————• 100%

Read these sentences then underline the correct word in *italics* in a and b.

They *always* work 16 hours a day.
They *rarely* take breaks.
They are *never* late.

a With all verbs except *be*, the adverb goes *before / after* the verb.
b With *be*, the adverb goes *before / after* the verb.

» For more information, go to **Grammar reference** on page 93.

5 Make true sentences about you. Use an adverb of frequency.
   Example: I ___often___ work ten hours a day.
1 I work ten hours a day.
2 I'm late for work.
3 I take breaks.
4 I work five days a week.
5 I'm sick and take a day off.

6 Work with a partner. Ask and answer questions about the sentences in **5**. Use an adverb in your answer.
   Example: A *Do you work ten hours a day?*
   B *No, I never work ten hours a day. I work …*

7 Find two questions in the article in **2**. What are the question words?

8 Answer the questions in *Language point 2*.

LANGUAGE POINT 2

Match questions 1–7 to answers a–g.
1 **Who** do the robots work for? ___   a Office products.
2 **What** does Staples deliver? ___   b After 16 hours.
3 **Where** do the robots work? ___   c To recharge their batteries.
4 **How often** do they take a day off? ___   d To move items.
5 **When** do they stop work? ___   e Never.
6 **Why** do they stop work? ___   f In the warehouse.
7 **How** does Staples use the robots? ___   g For Staples.

What do the question words in **bold** in 1–7 refer to?
a The way/method ___*How*___   e Places _____
b General information ___*What*___   f Reasons _____
c Time _____   g Frequency _____
d People _____

---

9 Work with a partner. Ask and answer questions about your company and your work. Use these prompts.
Who / work for?
What / produce or provide?
Where / work?
Why / like / your job?
When / start / work?
How often / take / day off?

>> For more exercises, go to **Practice file 4** on page 93.

Practically speaking | How to use sequencing words

1 ▶ 4.3 Listen to how the robots at Staples do their job. Number the stages a–e in the correct order 1–5.
a ___ the person takes the correct items for the order
b _1_ the warehouse computer receives customer orders
c ___ the robot returns the box and starts again
d ___ the robot finds the box and delivers it to a human co-worker
e ___ the computer tells a robot to find the correct box

2 ▶ 4.3 Listen again and match the words below to the five stages a–e in **1**.
Example: First of all, the warehouse computer receives customer orders.

first of all _b_   finally ___   after that ___   then ___   next ___

3 Think of stages for a process at work or your typical day. Tell your partner the stages with the sequencing words in **2**.
Example: First of all, I check emails. Then, I send new orders to the warehouse. Next, I …

Business communication | Asking for and offering help

1 Do you share files at work? How do you share them? Do you use file-sharing systems like Dropbox, Hightail, Google Drive, etc? What problems do you have when you share files?

2 ▶ 4.4 Listen to two colleagues, Nathan and Melissa. Underline the correct words in *italics*.

1 Nathan can't *log in to / log out of* his company's file-sharing system.
2 The password uses *lower-case letters / UPPER-CASE LETTERS*.
3 Nathan can't find the *meetings / project* folder.
4 Nathan *finds / doesn't find* the folder by using the search box.
5 You need to *log in / accept an invitation* to share the folder.
6 Nathan finds the email invitation in *his inbox / the file-sharing system*.
7 Nathan clicks on *view folder / share folder*.
8 Nathan *can / can't* see the folder now.

3 ▶ 4.4 Listen again. Number the expressions a–j in the order you hear them 1–10.

a Yes, of course. ___
b Do you want a hand? ___
c Can you help me? ___
d That would be great, thanks. ___
e I don't know how to do that. ___
f Sure. ___
g How do I do that? ___
h Yes, please. ___
i Can I help? _1_
j Can you give me a hand? ___

4 Work with a partner. Are the expressions in **3** asking for help (*A*), offering help (*O*) or responding (*R*)? Write the letter next to the expression.
   Example: Can you help me? A

>> For more exercises, go to **Practice file 4** on page 92.

5 You have a list of technical problems below. Move around the class and ask different people for help. Use the key expressions to find someone who can help you to:
   • log in to your company's Internet/intranet
   • download an app to your tablet
   • share a large file with a group of people
   • access a list of contacts at work
   • use the projector with your laptop
   • connect your smartphone to your computer

6 Work with a partner. Make a list of some other things you need help with at work. Then join another group and ask them for help.

Key expressions

Asking for help
Can you help me?
Can you give me a hand?
How do I ...?
I don't know how to ...

Responding to a request for help
Yes, of course.
Sure.

Offering help
Can I help?
Do you want/need a hand?

Responding to offers
Yes, please.
That would be great.
No, I'm OK, thanks.

Responding to thanks
You're welcome.

Making use of technology

Discussion

1 Look at the technology products A–F. What are they and what are they used for?

2 ▶ 4.5 Listen to six people talking about why they use the products in 1. Which products A–F are they talking about?

1 ___   2 ___   3 ___   4 ___   5 ___   6 ___

3 Which of the products in the pictures do you use? Are they useful? Write each product in the table below. Add other technology products that you use.

Very useful	Useful	Quite useful	A little useful	Not very useful	Not useful

4 Work with a partner and discuss your answers in 3. Give reasons for your answers.

5 Work in small groups. Discuss your answers in 3 and 4. Which is your group's favourite product?

Task

1 Work in small groups. Choose one of the topics below. Think of a new product or technology idea that can make our lives better in this area. What is it? Describe it, how it works and why it is useful.
- at home
- travelling/commuting
- health
- at work
- studying/learning
- communication
- free time / sport / hobbies
- sleeping
- food and drink

2 Present your idea to the rest of the class. While you listen to the other presentations, think of two questions to ask about their products.

3 Which idea is your favourite?

5 Communication

Starting point

1 What types of correspondence do you use in your job?

2 How many hours a day do you spend on correspondence and paperwork?

Tip | *fill in/out*

fill in (British English) = *fill out* (American English)

Working with words | Documents and correspondence

1 Does your company use lots of paper? Why is it a good idea to use less? Read about how to use less paper in an office. Which ideas does your company use?

IS THERE A MOUNTAIN OF PAPER IN YOUR OFFICE?

The average UK office worker uses 10,000 sheets of paper per year! This costs money to buy, use (e.g. print and photocopy), store and transport. UK businesses can spend more than one billion pounds per year on this. And using less paper saves time and trees, as well as money. It's easy to do:

THINK BEFORE YOU PRINT

Companies usually receive many **CV**s from people who want to work for them. If their CVs arrive by email, just save them on your company's computer system. If they arrive as hard copy by post, you can scan them and save them electronically. When you want to get new employees for your company, ask them to fill in online **application form**s.

SEND ELECTRONIC DOCUMENTS ONLY

You can send most documents electronically. When you order products, use an online electronic **order form**. Send your customers e-**invoice**s and e-receipts for payment. For example,

the UK supermarket Booths doesn't give receipts to some of its regular customers in the shop anymore – it just saves their receipt to their account online instead. When you deliver products, use e-**delivery note**s. And when you meet a new contact, send them a quick email or text message, instead of giving them a **business card**. You can even sign and send sales or employment **contract**s online.

MORE COMPUTER SCREENS, FEWER PRINTERS AND PHOTOCOPIERS

Have two computer screens on your desk so that you can look at two documents at the same time. Don't print a **hard copy** of office documents like meeting notes or reports – just attach them to an email, or upload them to your company's file-sharing system. If you need to keep copies of things like letters and **receipt**s, just scan them and save them. You don't need to photocopy and keep hard copies.

2 Can you think of more ideas to reduce the amount of paper we use at work?

3 What things do you need in these situations? Match the words in **bold** from the text in **1** with each situation.

1 You want to apply for a job. _____, _____

2 You want to get five new laptops for the sales team. _____

3 You want a record of your payment for lunch at a restaurant. _____

4 You meet a new client for the first time. _____

5 You send a customer a list of the items they ordered and the total price. _____

6 The delivery company brings you 20 boxes of paper for the photocopier. _____

7 Your boss wants to read your report. You need to print it. _____

8 You decide to start doing business with a new customer or supplier. _____

Tip | *copy*

Copy is a verb and a noun:
*I rarely **copy** reports.*
*We only have one **copy** of the report.*

4 Match the verbs from the text in **1** to the correct definitions a–h.

1 attach ___   a make a hard copy of an electronic document
2 print ___   b make something smaller in size or quantity
3 reduce ___   c add a document to an email
4 save ___   d make an electronic copy of a hard copy document
5 scan ___   e write your name on a document
6 sign ___   f keep a copy of an electronic document
7 upload ___   g write information in a form, e.g. order form
8 fill in ___   h put a document or file onto an online system

5 Which of the documents in **3** do you use at work? Which of the actions in **4** do you do with these documents?

> *Example: I attach **invoices** to emails and I **sign** new contracts.*

6 ▶5.1 Listen to a phone call between two colleagues.

1 What do they discuss? What is the problem?
2 What types of documents do they talk about?

7 ▶5.1 Listen again and write the nouns from the list next to verbs 1–7.

a hard copy   *an email* (x2)   *a folder*   *an order form*   *a document*   *an invoice*

1 receive _____
2 print _____
3 save _____
4 open _____
5 attach _____
6 send _____
7 forward _____

8 Look at the pictures. Match the verb + noun phrases in **7** with the correct pictures.

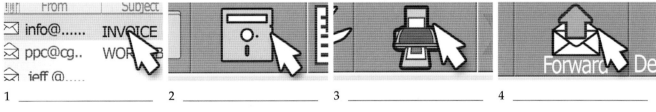

1 _____   2 _____   3 _____   4 _____

5 _____   6 _____   7 _____

≫ For more exercises, go to **Practice file 5** on page 94.

9 Work with a partner. Ask and answer questions about emails. **Student A**, turn to **page 111**. **Student B**, turn to **page 113**.

10 Work in small groups. Discuss these questions.

1 What kind of documents do you send by email at work? Do you send any documents by post?
2 How often do you check your emails at work? Do you check your work emails at the weekend?
3 Do you prefer to call or email to do the things below? Why?
   - Arrange to meet
   - Solve a problem
   - Find out information

Language at work | Past simple: *be* and regular verbs

1 ▶ 5.2 Listen to a conversation between Janusz and Carlos and choose the correct answers.

1 Janusz was at a *meeting / presentation* about branding.
2 It was at *breakfast / lunchtime* .
3 Carlos *was / wasn't* in the office yesterday.

2 ▶ 5.2 Listen again. Complete the conversation with *was, wasn't, were* or *weren't*.

Janusz Sorry I'm late. I ¹_____ at the presentation on branding.
Carlos Oh, ²_____ that this morning?
Janusz Yes, at 7.30 in the Century Hotel.
Carlos Oh. ³_____ it good?
Janusz Yes, the presentation ⁴_____ really interesting, and there ⁵_____ lots of good questions at the end.
Carlos ⁶_____ there many people there?
Janusz There ⁷_____ many people for the breakfast at the start, but there ⁸_____ lots for the presentation. It ⁹_____ too early for some people!
Carlos ¹⁰_____ you on time?
Janusz Of course! But the breakfast ¹¹_____ very good. Anyway, why ¹²_____ you in the office yesterday?
Carlos There ¹³_____ terrible problems with my flight back from Rome ...

3 Complete *Language point 1* about the past simple for *be*. Use *was, wasn't, were* and *weren't*.

Tip | Short forms

When speaking, use *wasn't/ weren't*:
He **wasn't** at the meeting today.
In formal or written English, use *was not / were not*:
The company CEO **was not** at the conference.

LANGUAGE POINT 1

Positive
I/He/She/It _____ late.
You/We/They _____ late.

Negative
I/He/She/It _____ late.
You/We/They _____ late.

Questions
_____ I/he/she/it late?
_____ you/we/they late?

Short answers
Yes, I/he/she/it _____.
No, I/he/she/it _____.
Yes, you/we/they _____.
No, you/we/they _____.

We can make negative questions with *wasn't* and *weren't*.
  Example: Why weren't you in the office yesterday? Wasn't your flight on time?

》 For more information, go to **Grammar reference** on page 95.

4 Work with a partner. Ask and answer questions about a report. **Student A, turn to page 111. Student B, turn to page 118.**

5 ▶ 5.3 Lydia calls Piotr about a presentation at an event. Look at Lydia's 'to do' list. Listen and tick (✓) the things that she did.

To do:
  * Call presenter Ron Peters ☐
  * Confirm the time of the presentation ☐
  * Call 'Century Hotel' ☐
  * Book the room ☐

6 ▶ 5.3 Listen again and complete these sentences using the past simple form of the verbs in brackets.
1 Sorry I _____ (miss) your call.
2 I _____ (want) to ask about the event.
3 _____ you _____ (call) Ron Peters?
4 I _____ (call) him yesterday.
5 What time _____ you _____ (decide) to start?
6 I _____ (invite) him to have lunch with us.
7 _____ you _____ (book) the hotel?
8 I _____ (phone) the Century Hotel.
9 I _____ (not/book) it.

>> For more exercises, go to **Practice file 5** on page 95.

7 Look at audio script 5.3. Complete *Language point 2* about the past simple for regular verbs. Use *did*, *didn't* and *-ed*.

LANGUAGE POINT 2

Positive
  I/He/She/It
  You/We/They verb + _____

Negative
  I/He/She/It
  You/We/They _____ + verb

Questions
  (What/Why/How) _____ I/
  he/she/it/you/we/they + verb?

Short answers
  Yes, I/he/she/it/you/we/they
  _____.

  No, I/he/she/it/you/we/they
  _____.

---

8 Work with a partner. Ask and answer questions about a phone message. **Student A**, turn to **page 112**. **Student B**, turn to **page 118**.

Practically speaking | How to apologize

1 When was the last time you said 'sorry'? Why did you say it?

2 ▶ 5.4 Listen to conversations 1–3. Match the problem with the reason in each one. Write 1, 2 or 3.

Problem	Reason
didn't phone the hotels ___	forgot ___
arrived late ___	was busy ___
didn't send the report ___	train was late ___

3 ▶ 5.4 Listen again and complete the apologies from the three conversations.
1 Hello. _____. My train was very late.
2 No, I didn't. _____. I was really busy yesterday.
3 Oh no! I forgot! _____. I'll do it now.

4 Work with a partner. Take turns to apologize in these situations. Give reasons.
- You are in a traffic jam and will be late for a job interview. Call the company.
- You couldn't email your boss a report because you had technical problems with your computer. Take him a hard copy and explain the problem.
- You weren't at the meeting this morning. Your manager asks you why.
- It's your team leader's birthday today. You talked to the team and you agreed to buy the cake, but you forgot. Speak to one of the team.
- A customer didn't receive a delivery because you made a mistake with their address. Call the customer.

Tip | *That's OK / No problem!*
Use *That's OK* or *No problem* to respond to an apology:
A *I'm really sorry I forgot your birthday.*
B **No problem!**

Business communication | Solving problems

1 Do you have these problems at work? Who normally solves them?
- late deliveries
- bad products or services
- machinery or equipment not working
- human mistakes
- angry customers

2 ▶ 5.5 Listen to a phone call. Which problems in **1** do they have?

3 ▶ 5.5 Listen again and complete the expressions from the conversation.
1 We _____ a problem with the order for Gosport.
2 We _____ all the baseball bats and T-shirts yesterday so I _____ ship them tomorrow. But the logos on the caps _____.
3 We _____ fix the machine today and print them again.
4 OK. _____ worry.
5 I know the Purchasing Manager at Gosport, so I _____ to him …
6 We _____ give another delivery date for this.
7 Sure. I _____ the factory now and I _____ you know as soon as I can.
8 That _____ be great. Thanks a lot.

>> For more exercises, go to **Practice file 5** on page 94.

4 Read this email from your boss.

> Dear both,
>
> I'm in meetings all day today, so can you deal with these between you, please?
>
> - Who is on Reception this week? (Where's Astrid?)
> - Gosport phoned. Purchasing says the invoice was wrong for the last order.
> - The new printers don't work with our computers. What can IT do about it?
> - Did someone book my tickets for Moscow? Remember I go next Monday.
> - Ellen in Sales leaves this week. Can we organize a leaving party on Friday? And a present?

Work with a partner. Discuss the problems in the emails. **Student A,** turn to **page 112. Student B,** turn to **page 118.**

5 Think of a problem at work this week. Explain it to your partner. Take turns to try and solve your partner's problem and promise action.

Key expressions

Explaining the problem
I've/We've got a problem with …
There are some problems with …
I/We can't …
We did X …, but Y didn't work.

Solving the problem
You/We need to …
We can …

Promising action
I'll … speak to … / explain the situation / call … / let you know as soon as I can

Responding and thanking
Don't worry.
That would be great.
Thanks a lot for your help.
No problem.

Money talks

More and more Japanese companies are deciding that English is the company language. Company employees need to be able to communicate with international colleagues in meetings and in emails to help them expand their business outside Japan.

The Rakuten group introduced an 'English-only' policy in 2010. Now all company meetings, presentations, documents and emails are in English – even the signs in the company head office in Tokyo! English is also the company language at Fast Retailing (the parent company of clothing retailer Uniqlo) and the company wants to employ more non-Japanese people in its head office. The Honda Motor Company says that by 2020 top managers must speak English. And the CEO of another large motor industry company, Bridgestone, said that all new employees need to speak English to do well in the future.

To help their employees speak English, many of these companies provide English lessons. And the Japanese mobile phone company Softbank even offered one million yen (about $11,200) to employees who got a high score on their English test!

Discussion

1 Read the text. Which Japanese companies currently use English as the company language? Why?

2 ▶ 5.6 Listen to an expert talking about English-only policies at Japanese companies. What are the advantages and disadvantages of using English as the company language?

3 Can you think of more advantages and disadvantages for companies with an 'English-only' policy?

4 Do you think this is a good idea for these Japanese companies? Why/Why not?

5 How much of your company's work is in English? How many people at your company speak English?

Task

1 Work in small groups. Have a meeting to decide how to use an 'English-only' policy in your company. Decide the following:

1 When you must use English – all the time/only with foreign contacts/in all emails/only in meetings?

2 Who must use English – all employees or only some people?

3 What documents must be in English.

4 How you can help employees improve their English.

2 After the meeting, present your ideas to the class.

6 Networking

Starting point

1 What different ways of communicating with colleagues do you use in your company?

2 Does your company use social media to communicate with its employees or customers?

Working with words | Social media and networking

1 Match the social networking sites with descriptions 1–4. Which sites do you use?

LinkedIn   Twitter   Facebook   Google+

1 The biggest social **network**. People connect with their friends and family and **share** information with them in **a post**. You can **comment on** other people's posts or click on 'like' to show that you like them. People you are connected with are called your friends.

2 People use this social network to connect with friends or with other people with the same interests. You can make groups (called circles) of people to share with.

3 People use this site to build **professional** networks. Users write a **profile** and **connect with** other people in their business area. These people are then called your connections. People share information about work topics and comment on it or 'like' it.

4 People use this site **to post** short messages called tweets. If you want to see everything someone posts, you can follow them.

2 Match the words in **bold** in 1 to definitions 1–8.
1 connected with your job _____
2 a group or system of connected things _____
3 to write something online so that other people can read it _____
4 what somebody has written on social media _____
5 a description of a person or organization _____
6 to create a relationship with somebody _____
7 to show or tell something to other people online _____
8 to write a note giving your opinion on something _____

Tip | post

Post is a verb and a noun:
*My company **posts** something on our Facebook page almost every day.* (verb)
*Today's **post** was about our new product.* (noun)

3 Look at the graph. Which social networks do most people use to find a job? Which sites do most employers use? Do you use social media to find a job?

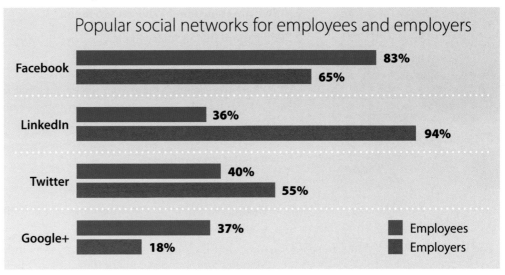

Popular social networks for employees and employers

Facebook 83% / 65%
LinkedIn 36% / 94%
Twitter 40% / 55%
Google+ 37% / 18%

■ Employees
■ Employers

4 ▶ 6.1 Listen to the interview with an expert on how to use social media to get a job. Tick (✓) the things the expert talks about.

your profile ☐
your timeline ☐
adding contacts ☐
joining groups ☐
your Google+ circles ☐
your status updates ☐

5 ▶ 6.1 Listen again and use the words from the list to complete the sentences.

join   add (x2)   *update* (x2)   *on   build*

1 I'm _____ Twitter and LinkedIn.
2 You need to _____ your profile regularly.
3 _____ a link to an online CV.
4 You _____ contacts to _____ your network.
5 _____ your status, that means post something, regularly.
6 _____ a group conversation or a Twitter chat.

6 Use the words from the list to complete the questions.

'like'   share   join   to follow   search for
comment on   update (x2)   *tweet*

When did you last …?

1 _____ your social network profile
2 _____ your Facebook or LinkedIn status
3 _____ or _____ something on social media
4 send a _____ on Twitter
5 _____ a social networking group
6 _____ a photo on social media
7 start _____ someone on Twitter
8 _____ somebody on social media

》 For more exercises, go to **Practice file 6** on page 96.

7 Work with a partner. Ask and answer the questions in **6**.

8 Work with a partner. Talk about how your company can use social media to:

• find new staff, new customers and new suppliers
• promote new products, advertise events, increase sales

Language at work | Past simple: irregular verbs | Time expressions

1 What are trade fairs? Who goes to them?

2 Read about this Industry Expo.
1 What type of industry was it for?
2 When and where was it?
3 Where were manufacturers, suppliers and other representatives from?
4 Does your business or industry have similar events?

✉

Subject: Recent events

Textile Industry Expo Date: 1–4 August

Venue: Ho Chi Minh City International Exhibition and Convention Center, Vietnam

Almost 100 companies went to this year's Industry Expo. Manufacturers and suppliers from China, the Republic of Korea and India met Vietnamese producers, and two companies from Austria and Italy also had representatives at the event.

Don't miss this event next year. **Click here for early registration.**

---

3 There are three verbs in the description of the Expo. <u>Underline</u> them. Do they describe the past or present?

4 ▶ 6.2 Listen to Giang and Enzo meet at the Expo.
1 Where is Enzo from?
2 What do they give each other?
3 How did they travel to the Expo?

5 ▶ 6.2 Listen again. Number these verbs in the order you hear them 1–7.
came ___   took _1_   flew ___   had ___   were ___   left ___   met ___

6 Answer the questions in the *Language point*.

LANGUAGE POINT

Write the verbs in **3** and **5** next to the infinitive.
1 be – ___*was*___   5 have – _____
2 take – _____   6 leave – _____
3 go – _____   7 come – _____
4 meet – _____   8 fly – _____

Read this extract from Enzo and Giang's conversation. Complete the timeline with the time expressions in **bold**.

*I came to Ho Chi Minh City **last night**, but I left Bologna **two days ago**. I flew to Milan and then to Shanghai. I had a day in Shanghai, so I met some colleagues there **yesterday**.*

a year ago   last month   _____   _____   _____   this morning
●————————●————————●————————●————————●————————●

» For more information, go to **Grammar reference** on page 97.

7 Work with a partner. Describe your last trip. Talk about some of the following and use time expressions:
- where you went
- how long the journey was
- when you left/arrived
- when you came home
- what meeting (conference) you had
- where you left from
- who you met

8 ▶ 6.3 Listen to Giang ask Enzo about his career. Complete these questions.
1 How did you _____ a sales manager in textiles?
2 Why did you _____?
3 When did you _____ your current company?

9 ▶ 6.3 Listen again. What are Enzo's answers?

》 For more exercises, go to **Practice file 6** on page 97.

10 Work with a partner.
1 Write five sentences about your career using time expressions.
   Example: I went to university in 1999.
   I studied …
2 Swap your sentences. Ask and answer questions about your careers. Begin with the question: *How did you become a … (job title)?*

Practically speaking | How to describe a trip

1 ▶ 6.4 Mike talks about his trip to Brussels. Listen and tick (✓) the adjectives you hear.

Adjectives	Mike's trip	+ / – / N
nice		
OK		
fine		
delicious		
interesting		
good		
terrible		
tiring		
comfortable		
long		

2 Are the adjectives in **1** positive (+), negative (–) or neutral (N)? Write +, – or N next to the adjectives.

3 Which of the adjectives in **1** can describe …
- a hotel
- a journey
- a city or country
- a meal or the food
- a presentation

4 Work with a partner. Look at some pictures from a trip. Take turns to ask and answer questions. **Student A**, turn to **page 112**. **Student B**, turn to **page 119**.

5 Now ask your partner about their most recent trip.
   Example: How was the flight? How was the hotel? Was the food OK?

Business communication | Making conversation

1 How can you start a conversation in these two situations?
  1 You're at a conference cocktail party. It's the end of the first day.
  2 You arrive at your company. You see a visitor in Reception.

2 ▶6.5 ▶6.6 Listen to two conversations and match them to the correct situations in **1**.

3 ▶6.5 Match expressions 1–8 to responses a–h. Then listen again and check.
  1 Can I join you? ___
  2 I hear you work for GST. ___
  3 My name's Simon Turing. ___
  4 What do you think of the conference? ___
  5 Do you come here every year? ___
  6 Do you know a lot of people here? ___
  7 Would you like another drink? ___
  8 Please excuse me. ___

  a Very interesting.
  b Sure. See you later, maybe.
  c Yes, of course.
  d No, not many.
  e Pleased to meet you.
  f No, thanks. I'm fine.
  g Yes, that's right.
  h No, this is my first time.

4 Work with a partner. You are at a conference. Practise this conversation:
  • start the conversation
  • talk about the conference
  • offer something
  • end the conversation

5 ▶6.6 Work with a partner. Think of possible responses to these sentences. Then listen again and compare your answers.
  1 Can I help you?
  2 Is this your first time here?
  3 Please go in and take a seat.
  4 Can I get you something?
  5 Nice talking to you.

>> For more exercises, go to **Practice file 6** on page 96.

6 Work with a partner. Practise this conversation:
  • start a conversation with a visitor in Reception
  • offer to take him/her to a colleague's office
  • offer something to drink
  • end the conversation

7 Work with a partner. Practise making conversation. **Student A**, turn to **page 113. Student B**, turn to **page 118.**

Key expressions

Starting a conversation
Can I join you?
I hear you work for ...
Is this your first time ...?
What do you think of ...?

Offering
Can I help you?
Can I get you something?
Would you like another ...?
Please take a seat.
Please go in and take a seat.

Responding
Yes, please.
Yes, of course.
Yes, that's right.
No, thanks. (I'm fine.)

Finishing a conversation
Please excuse me.
Nice talking to you.
See you later.

The networking game

Play the networking game with your partner.

Choose a square.
On a blue square, read the question or sentence, and then respond.
On an orange square, read the answer and ask an appropriate question.
If you are right, you win the square.
Then your partner chooses a square and does the same.
Try to complete a line of five squares across ➡, down ⬇ or diagonally ↘ before your partner.

| Examples: | **Do you know Ali?** | *You say:* *No. Pleased to meet you, Ali.* | | **Do ...?** No, not many. | *You say:* *Do you know many people here?* |

Is this ...? No, I was here last year.	**Where did you go on your last business trip?**	**How ...?** Fine. There was no traffic on the roads.	**When did you join your company?**	**Can I ... coffee?** Yes, please.
My name's Rudolf.	**Can ...?** Yes, sure. Take a seat.	**I hear ...** Yes, it's a great company.	**Nice talking to you.**	**Can I find you on Facebook?**
What ...? It's very interesting.	**Would ...?** No, thanks. I'm fine.	**Please excuse me.**	**... the presentation?** It was very interesting.	**How was the weekend?**
Does your company use social media?	**How ...?** It was delicious.	**Do you use social media for work?**	**How ...?** My room was a bit small, but it was very comfortable.	**Do you follow anyone on Twitter?**
How did you become a ... (your job)?	**When did you first join social media?**	**Do ...?** No, not every year, but I was here last year.	**How many social media friends do you have?**	**Can ...?** Yes, please. I have a lot of bags.

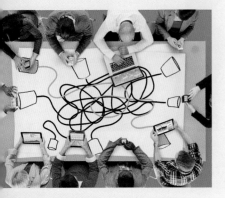

Focus

1 How do you normally communicate with people in your job? Tick (✓) the words in the list. Discuss your answers with a partner.

Phone	☐	Twitter	☐
Face-to-face meetings	☐	Email	☐
Skype	☐	Videoconference	☐
Text	☐	Facebook	☐
Teleconference	☐	Other	☐ _____

2 Ask your partner how much time they spend communicating in these ways.

Example: How much time do you spend in meetings every day or every week?
How much time do you spend on email per day?

3 ▶01 Watch four people talking about communication at work. Make notes about their answers in the table.

	Speaker 1	Speaker 2	Speaker 3	Speaker 4
How do you normally communicate with people at work?				
How much time do you spend communicating in these ways?				

4 Compare your notes in **3** with a partner.

Communicating by email

5 Think about how you use email. Complete these sentences with numbers or underline the words in *italics*. Then compare your sentences with a partner.

1 I have _____ email accounts.
2 I send about _____ emails per day. I get about _____ emails per day.
3 I spend about _____ hours per week checking my emails.
4 I *often / sometimes / rarely* change my email password.

6 ▶02 Watch a video about email communication and answer questions 1–4. Are the answers similar to your answers in **5**?

1 How many email accounts do most people have?
2 How many emails does the average business person send per day?
3 How many hours a week do people spend checking emails?
4 How often do most people change their password?

7 ▶02 Watch the video again. Make notes about the numbers in the table.

Number	Notes
3 billion	*email accounts in the world*
150 billion	
90 billion	
30%	
1971	
1991	
1998	
75%	
123456	
29%	
20 million	

Business writing

8 Read and compare two emails. Match the emails (A or B) to sentences 1–6.
One sentence is true for both emails.

1 The sender knows the receiver very well. ___
2 More than one person received the email. ___
3 It is formal and polite. ___
4 It is informal and friendly. ___
5 The sender wants a reply. ___
6 The sender wants a meeting. ___

Email A

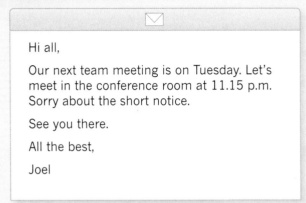

Hi all,

Our next team meeting is on Tuesday. Let's meet in the conference room at 11.15 p.m. Sorry about the short notice.

See you there.

All the best,

Joel

Email B

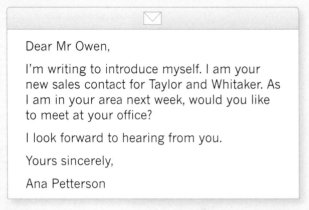

Dear Mr Owen,

I'm writing to introduce myself. I am your new sales contact for Taylor and Whitaker. As I am in your area next week, would you like to meet at your office?

I look forward to hearing from you.

Yours sincerely,

Ana Petterson

9 Look at the two emails in **8** again. Complete the table using expressions from the emails.

	More friendly and less formal	More formal and polite
Starting the email	Hello	2 _____
	1 _____	
Give the reason for writing	It's about …	With regard to …
		3 _____
Arrange a meeting	Do you want to meet at …?	5 _____
	4 _____	
Apologize	Sorry, but …	I apologize that …
Future contact	6 _____	7 _____
End the email	Bye for now	Best regards
	8 _____	9 _____

10 Write two emails. Use the expressions from the table in **9**.

1 An email to two colleagues. You want a meeting tomorrow.
2 An email to a new customer. Ask for a meeting.

7 Departments

Starting point

1 How many departments does your company have? Can you name them?

2 Which department has a large number of employees? Which is a small department?

3 What does your department do?

Working with words | Departments and responsibilities

1 Match the names of the departments with pictures a–h.

Logistics   Finance   Sales   IT (Information Technology)
R&D (Research and Development)   HR (Human Resources)
Marketing   Customer Services

a _____

b _____

c _____

d _____

e _____

f _____

g _____

h _____

2 Read the article about jobs at Komancom. Complete the sentences with four of the department names from **1**.

CAREER PROFILES

Find out about a career with Komancom. Read about some of the people who work for us around the world.

Cameron Torres works in the ¹_____ Department in Argentina. He has meetings with customers, and **contacts** them by phone and email to **develop** good business relationships.

Bud Cardoso works in the ²_____ Department in Brazil. He **checks** financial information and **deals with** accounts. He likes working with numbers.

Adel Sharma works in the ³_____ Department in India. She **promotes** products so that more people know about them. Her department **supports** the Sales Department.

Esma Demir works in the ⁴_____ Department in Turkey. She**'s responsible for** the warehouse. She contacts suppliers and **organizes** deliveries. It is important that the deliveries are on time.

3 There are two verbs in **bold** in each profile. Match them to definitions 1–8. Change the form of the verb if necessary.

1 make something bigger and/or more successful _____
2 help someone with something _____
3 be in charge of something _____
4 communicate with someone _____
5 say good things about something to help sell it _____
6 arrange something _____
7 confirm that something is correct _____
8 work with something or someone _____

4 Underline the correct verbs in *italics*.

1 I'm in the Customer Services Department. Customers *support / contact* me every day and I *deal with / 'm responsible for* their questions and problems.
2 The IT Department *develops / is responsible for* the computers in all the offices.
3 The R&D Department *organizes / develops* new products and the Production Department makes them.
4 I work with Guilherme in the Finance Department. Sometimes he asks me to *check / support* his work for him. He doesn't want to make any mistakes!
5 The Marketing Department *checks / promotes* the products.
6 In the HR Department we *contact / support* the employees and *organize / check* the recruitment of new staff.

5 Work with a partner. Make sentences about these departments using words in the table.

Logistics	is responsible for	suppliers
Finance	deals with	customers
Sales	develops	information
IT	checks	employees
R&D	organizes	deliveries
HR	contacts	products
Marketing	promotes	accounts
Customer Services	supports	computers

Example: The Logistics Department organizes deliveries.

>> For more exercises, go to **Practice file 7** on page 98.

6 ▶ 7.1 We can pronounce the -s at the end of words as /s/, /z/ or /ɪz/. Listen to the examples then write the sounds you hear for the word endings below.

Example: works /s/   *is* /z/   *organizes* /ɪz/

deals ____   resources ____   promotes ____
checks ____   departments ____   employees ____
contacts ____   computers ____   services ____

7 Work with a partner. Ask them about their job using the words from **5** and **6** and your own ideas. Then tell another group about your partner's job.

Example: Elaine works in the Accounts Department. She deals with invoices and checks accounts …

8 Take turns to describe some departments in your company. Try to guess the department your partner describes.

Example: **A** This department deals with customers.
B Sales.
A Correct.

Tip | Word building

When you learn a new word, you can make more words with it:

develop – developer, development
produce – products, production
organize – organizer, organization
deliver – delivery

Language at work | Prepositions of place and movement

1 Jim Berman plans to visit Olivia Gonzalez's company. Read Olivia's email to Jim. Look at the map and find one mistake in her directions.

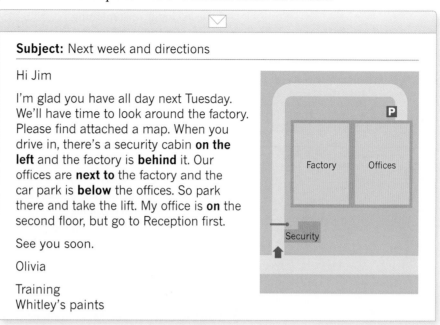

Subject: Next week and directions

Hi Jim

I'm glad you have all day next Tuesday. We'll have time to look around the factory. Please find attached a map. When you drive in, there's a security cabin **on the left** and the factory is **behind** it. Our offices are **next to** the factory and the car park is **below** the offices. So park there and take the lift. My office is **on** the second floor, but go to Reception first.

See you soon.

Olivia

Training
Whitley's paints

Tip | British and American English

British and American English have some vocabulary differences:

British English | American English
ground floor/first floor
toilet/restroom
lift/elevator

2 Look at the office plan below. <u>Underline</u> the correct words in *italics* in 1–6.
1 Production is on the *left / right* of Reception.
2 Finance is *above / below* HR.
3 The MD's office is *between / next to* the conference room.
4 The cafeteria is on the *second / third* floor.
5 The car park is *in front of / below* Reception.
6 R&D is *in / between* Reception and Production.

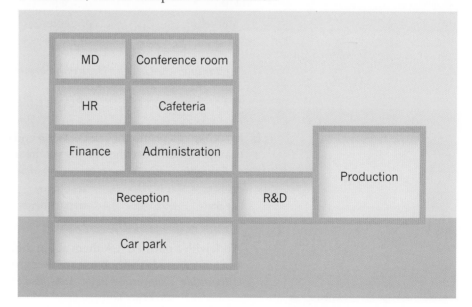

3 Work with a partner. Look at two office plans. **Student A,** turn to **page 113.** **Student B,** turn to **page 119.**

4 Work with a partner. Describe where rooms and departments are in your company. Where is your office?

5 ▶ 7.2 Jim arrives at the security cabin. Listen and complete the security man's directions.
You go [1]_____ this road and turn right. Go [2]_____ the factory to the offices, but don't park there. Look for the car park sign and drive [3]_____ below the offices and go [4]_____ the car park there.

6 Use the prepositions in **2** and **5** to complete the *Language point*.

LANGUAGE POINT

Match the prepositions of place in **2** to diagrams 1–8.

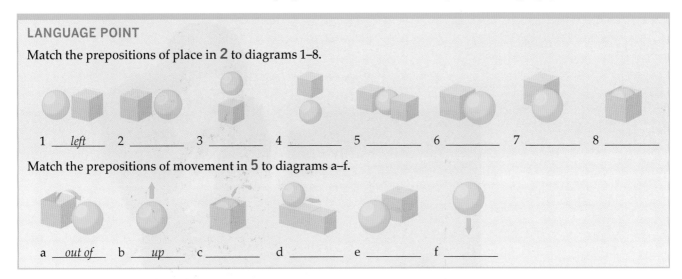

1 ___*left*___ 2 _____ 3 _____ 4 _____ 5 _____ 6 _____ 7 _____ 8 _____

Match the prepositions of movement in **5** to diagrams a–f.

a ___*out of*___ b ___*up*___ c _____ d _____ e _____ f _____

>> For more information, go to **Grammar reference** on page 99.

7 Work with a partner. Take turns to give directions from where you are now to these places. Guess which place your partner gives directions to.

*Reception   the cafeteria   the lifts or stairs   your favourite café
the bank   your car   the train station   a cinema*

   Example: *Go past the lift and turn left …*

>> For more exercises, go to **Practice file 7** on page 99.

Tip | Giving directions and instructions

Use the imperative form of the verb to give directions and instructions:
Go along *this road.*
Enter *your password.*
Sometimes we use *You* + verb to be more polite:
You go along *this road and turn left.*

Practically speaking | How to use *this*, *that*, *these* and *those*

1 ▶ 7.3 Listen to four short conversations. Match each conversation 1–4 with a picture A–D.

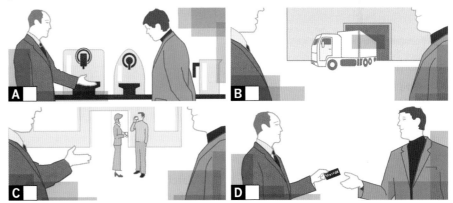

2 ▶ 7.3 Listen again and complete the short conversations.

1 A _____ is your visitor's pass.
  B Thanks very much.
2 A _____ are two of my colleagues.
  B Can you introduce me?
3 A _____ are our new products.
  B They look great.
4 A What is _____ building?
  B It's the warehouse.

3 Work with a partner. Draw a picture or map of your company or office. Ask and answer questions about the pictures or maps.

   Example: **A** *What's that?*   **B** *This is …*
            A *What are those?*   **B** *These are …*

Business communication | Leaving phone messages

1 ▶7.4 Listen to two phone calls. What mistakes does the receiver make?

2 ▶7.4 Listen again. How do the callers correct the information?

1 _____

2 _____

3 Work with a partner. Call your partner and check and correct details. **Student A**, turn to **page 113**. **Student B**, turn to **page 118**.

4 ▶7.5 Listen to a phone call. Complete the message.

MESSAGE FOR:	*Teresa Baum*
FROM:	
CALLING ABOUT:	
PHONE NUMBER:	
CALL BACK? ☐	
URGENT? ☐	

5 ▶7.5 Match 1–9 to a–i. Then listen again and check.

1 Could I speak ___
2 I'm sorry, but ___
3 Could I leave ___
4 It's ___
5 So ___
6 Can she call ___
7 Can I have ___
8 Is that ___
9 I'll give her ___

a your message.
b a contact number?
c a message for her?
d right?
e that's A-N-D-A-C.
f to Teresa Baum, please?
g Richard Andac.
h she isn't here this morning.
i me back as soon as possible?

>> For more exercises, go to **Practice file 7** on page 98.

6 Work with a partner. Practise leaving messages. **Student A**, turn to **page 113**. **Student B**, turn to **page 119**.

Key expressions

Asking to speak to someone
Could I speak to ...?
I'd like to speak to ...
Is ... there?

Leaving a message
Could I leave a message?
My number is ...
Can she call me back (as soon as possible)?

Taking a message
I'm sorry, but she isn't here/ available.
Can I take a message?
Can I have a contact number?
I'll give him/her your message.

Checking details
So that's ...
Is that right?

Correcting details
No, it's N as in New York / O as in Oslo.

Designing the perfect workspace

In 2005, the Czech branch of the pharmaceuticals company Pfizer moved into its new offices. The original offices didn't have many meeting spaces, so it was difficult for teams and departments to work well together. The new offices are a better place for teams and communication. Inside, there are a lot of open spaces for employees to meet and talk: coffee areas, meeting rooms, etc. The staff cafeteria seats 100 people and has a garden which can be used for meetings, too. The offices, though, are small, so people can concentrate when they need to. Communication between the departments was also very important. So the Medical, Marketing and Sales Departments are connected by stairs and small meeting areas between the floors. Altogether, the new offices are a comfortable place to work, with a balance of open spaces for good communication and small spaces for individual work.

Discussion

1 How are Pfizer's new offices different from the old ones?

2 Do the staff work in big or small offices?

3 How does the design help departments to work together?

4 What is your workspace like? Do you have a lot of open spaces? Are the different departments well located?

Task

1 Work in small groups. Talk about your company. Who is responsible for what? Who works with who? Who needs to communicate with who? How is your office/department designed?

2 Design your perfect office or workspace so everyone can do their job well and communicate easily with their colleagues.

3 Present your new workspace to the rest of the class.

8 Employment

Starting point

1 How many employees are there in your company/department/office?

2 How does your company recruit new employees? Does it have a human resources department?

Working with words | Employment

1 Read these job adverts.
1 What type of company is it?
2 Find two words that mean the same as *job*.
3 Which job needs a particular skill? What is it?

We are currently offering three positions for the right people:

Summer placement

Are you an **energetic** student with ambition? Get some work experience this summer. Every June–August we employ a **friendly** young person to help in our offices. Learn new skills and earn some money.

Web editor

We are looking for an **imaginative** but **focused** web editor to join our team. You are a **practical** person who can deal with problems on your own.

Website production assistant

This post needs a **careful** and **patient** person with basic skills in HTML. You assist **experienced** web producers and receive training.

Click here for more details.

2 Match the adjectives in **bold** in 1 to definitions 1–8.
1 thinks about things and does not make mistakes _____
2 can deal with everyday problems _____
3 has new and exciting ideas _____
4 very active and lots of energy _____
5 can work on one job for a long time _____
6 kind and helpful _____
7 has lots of skills and knowledge in the job _____
8 can wait for a long time _____

3 ▶8.1 Listen to these words. Write the number of syllables and <u>underline</u> the stress.

energetic _4_   imaginative ___   careful ___   friendly   ___
practical ___   focused   ___   patient ___   experienced ___

▶8.1 Now listen again and repeat the words.

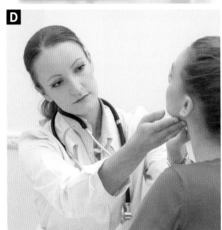

4 Work with a partner. Take turns to choose adjectives from **1** to describe the jobs in pictures A–F above. You can use more than one adjective. Guess what job your partner describes.

5 ▶ 8.2 Listen to Anton and Sandra in the HR Department of the company in **1**. They are discussing candidates for the jobs. Make notes about Monica and Roberto in the table.

	Monica	Roberto
Personal qualities	*friendly*	
Current situation		
Skills and experience		
Qualifications		

6 ▶ 8.2 Listen again and match 1–5 to a–e.

1 She has a lot ____
2 She's good ____
3 He has a ____
4 He doesn't have ____
5 He isn't very ____

a good at working on his own.
b of experience in book editing.
c any experience in editing.
d qualification in IT.
e at editing websites.

>> For more exercises, go to **Practice file 8** on page 100.

Tip | *experience in + -ing*
Use the -ing form after *experience in*:
*She has a lot of **experience in** book edit**ing**.*

7 Work with a partner. Tell your partner about your job.
1 What qualities do you need to do your job?
2 What skills, experience and qualifications do you have?

8 Present the information about your partner to another group.

Language at work | Present continuous

1 ▶ 8.3 Listen to two conversations in an office. Why are the people busy at the moment?

2 ▶ 8.3 Listen again. Complete the conversations using the words in brackets.

1　A　Where's Chantelle?
　　B　She ¹_____ (not work) in the office today. She ²_____ (work) at home.
　　A　Why ³_____ (she / do) that?
　　B　She ⁴_____ (finish) her report. Her boss wants it for 7.30 tomorrow morning.
2　A　Where are Bill and Sofia?
　　B　They ⁵_____ (do) the training course for that new finance software.
　　A　⁶_____ (they / do) the course all day?
　　B　No, ⁷_____ (they / not be). It's only a half-day course.

3 Answer the questions in the *Language point*.

LANGUAGE POINT

The verbs in **2** are in the present continuous tense. Which two of the following things do we use the present continuous tense for?
- An action or event in progress now
- An action or event in progress around the time of speaking
- A general fact or regular action

Look at the information about how we form the present continuous. Complete the information with examples from the conversations in **2**.

Positive
I am + verb + -*ing*.
You/We/They are + verb + -*ing*. ***Example:*** _____
He/She/It is + verb + -*ing*. ***Examples:*** _____ , _____ .

Negative
I'm not (am not) + verb + -*ing*.
You/We/They aren't (are not) + verb + -*ing*.
He/She/It isn't (is not) + verb + -*ing*. ***Example:*** _____

Questions
(Question word) am I + verb + -*ing*?
(Question word) are you/we/they + verb + -*ing*? ***Example:*** _____
(Question word) is he/she/it + verb + -*ing*? ***Example:*** _____

Short answers
Yes, I am.
No, I'm not.
Yes, you/we/they are.
No, you/we/they aren't. ***Example:*** _____
Yes, he/she/it is.
No, he/she/it isn't.

》 For more information, go to **Grammar reference** on page 101.

4 Match questions 1–5 to answers a–e.

1　What are you doing at the moment? ___
2　Are you working on any interesting projects? ___
3　How are your English lessons? ___
4　Could you give me a hand? ___
5　What is the weather like today? ___

a　It's raining.
b　Sorry. I'm trying to finish these plans.
c　I'm working with our partners in Italy.
d　Yes, we're working on a new hospital in Cairo.
e　They're difficult, but I'm making progress.

5 Work with a partner. Ask and answer questions 1–5 in **4**, giving answers that are true for you.

6 Read the article about our changing world of work.
   1 <u>Underline</u> all the examples of the present continuous.
   2 Do the present continuous verbs describe a changing or not-changing situation?

What is shaping our working world⟨?⟩

Computers are continuing to affect our employment in the twenty-first century. Mobile technology allows us to work on the move, as well as at home. But what else is shaping our working lives in this century?

- Employees aren't staying in the same jobs for long. Nowadays, the average employee moves to a new job every three years.

- The number of women in work is rising and more and more women are working in higher positions in companies.

- Many people are deciding their own working hours. Some people now work longer days but only four days a week, so more people are enjoying a longer weekend for the same amount of pay!

---

7 Do you agree with the article? Is it true for you and your company?
Tell the class.

>> For more exercises, go to **Practice file 8** on page 101.

8 Make a list of current changes where you work.
   Example: *employ more staff / spend more on training / invest in research / develop new products*

9 Work with a partner. Tell your partner about the changes using the present continuous. Try to give reasons for the changes.
   Example: *We're employing more staff at the moment because we're receiving more orders.*

Practically speaking | How to tell the time

1 ▶ 8.4 Listen to four conversations. Match conversations 1–4 to the times on the clocks A–D.

A ___   B ___   C ___   D ___

2 Work with a partner. Ask and answer these questions.
   1 What time did you start work today?
   2 What time do you normally have lunch?
   3 What time is it now?

3 Ask your partner three more *What time ...?* questions.

Tip | *at/on*

Use the prepositions *at* and *on* with times and days of the week:
*I start work **at** eight o'clock.*
*Can we meet **on** Tuesday at three o'clock?*

Business communication | Arranging to meet

1 When are you free this week? When are you busy?

2 ▶ 8.5 A company has a plan for more staff to work from home. Kasia wants to arrange a meeting with the heads of department, Bruno, Dolores and Chen. She calls Bruno first. Listen to the conversation. Put a cross (✗) when Kasia and Bruno are busy.

Thursday

	Kasia	Bruno
0800–0900		
0900–1000		
1000–1100		
1100–1200		
1200–1300		
1300–1400		
1400–1500		

3 ▶ 8.5 Listen again and complete these sentences.

1 We need to _____ _____ the plan …
2 _____ we _____ a meeting on Thursday …?
3 _____ two o'clock _____ for you?
4 Sorry, I'm _____ _____.
5 _____ _____ the morning?
6 What time _____ you _____?
7 9.30 is _____ _____ _____.
8 I _____ _____ between 8.00 and 10.00.
9 _____ you _____ after _____?
10 Dolores and I _____ an _____ at 12.00, so _____ _____ before that.
11 _____ 10.15 _____ _____ _____?
12 A quarter past ten on Thursday is _____.

4 Match 1–8 to a–h to make sentences and questions.

1 What time ___
2 Ten o'clock is ___
3 Can we arrange ___
4 Are you ___
5 Sorry, I'm ___
6 We need to ___
7 What about ___
8 Is 2.30 ___

a a meeting on Wednesday?
b busy in the afternoon?
c busy then.
d meet about the marketing plan.
e three o'clock?
f fine for me.
g OK for you?
h are you free?

» For more exercises, go to **Practice file 8** on page 100.

5 Work with a partner and arrange the meeting with Dolores.
Student A: you are Kasia. Call Dolores about the meeting on Thursday.
Student B: you are Dolores. Turn to **page 116**.

6 Now arrange the meeting with Chen.
Student A: you are Chen. Turn to **page 114**.
Student B: you are Bruno. Call Chen about the meeting.

7 Work in small groups. Arrange times this week for you all to:
- have a three-hour meeting
- have an extra English lesson
- interview people for the new receptionist position (two half days)

Key expressions

Asking to meet
Can we arrange a meeting?
We need to meet about …
I'd like to meet …

Asking about times
Is … OK?
Is … good for you?
What time are you free?
Are you free on/at …?
Can we meet on/at …?
Are you busy …?

Saying when you are free
… is good/fine for me.
I'm free on/at …

Saying when you are busy
Sorry, I'm busy then. I'm meeting …
I can't meet …

The right person for the job

Work with a partner. Your company is advertising two new jobs. You need to find the right person for the jobs. Follow stages 1 to 5 to find the right candidate.

STAGE 1 The job advert

Complete these notes to describe the type of person you are looking for in each job.

Marketing assistant
Experience:
Qualities:

Administrative assistant
Experience:
Qualities:

STAGE 2 Arranging the interviews

The job advert is written. You now need to arrange a day for interviews. Find a day when you are both free to interview people.

Student A, turn to **page 114**.
Student B, turn to **page 119**.

STAGE 3 Preparing for the interview

With your partner, create two short candidate profiles for each job, for example, experience and knowledge needed for the job.
Decide on some questions you want to ask.

STAGE 4 Holding the interviews

Join with another pair. Take turns to interview each person in the other pair for the job.

STAGE 5 Choosing the candidate

Go back to your first partner.
Discuss each candidate and decide which one to choose for the job.

9 Competition

Working with words | Competition

1 When you choose a hotel, which of these things are most important? Are any other factors important for you?

- Price
- Size
- Choice and range
- Staff
- Technology
- Quality
- Services
- Location

2 Which of the things in **1** do you think are important for hotels to be competitive?

3 ▶9.1 Listen to a hotel manager talking about the hotel group Accor. Tick (✓) the things in **1** which the manager mentions.

4 ▶9.1 Listen again and complete the table.

Hotel chain	Market segment	Description	Location
Motel 6	1_____	2_____ option	North America
All Seasons	3_____	good service, 4_____ staff	Asia Pacific
Novotel	5_____	6_____ quality, modern, 7_____ business facilities, easy to find	Worldwide
Sofitel	Top range	five star 8_____, special experience	Worldwide

5 Work with a partner. Discuss which things in **1** are important for your company and your competitors. Does your company offer something special?

6 Complete sentences 1–6 with the words from the list.

wide   competitive   comfort   expensive   budget   mid-range   market

1 The hotel industry is very _____ – there are a lot of big chains out there.
2 They are the only international group with hotels in every _____ segment.
3 This means they can offer all their customers a _____ choice.
4 Their _____ hotels offer the customer a low-price option.
5 Their _____ segment hotels offer more _____ and better services.
6 Their top-range hotels are _____, but each one gives the customer a special experience.

7 Work with a partner. Talk about a hotel or other company you use (for example, IT company or office supplies company). Why do you use them? Use adjectives and nouns from the table to describe them.

Adjectives	Nouns
budget/economy/mid-range	market segment
low/high	prices
good/bad	choice and range
cheap/expensive	location
fast/slow	technology/facilities
up-to-date/modern	quality
wide	service
friendly	staff

Example: I use the [name] hotel chain. They have cheap prices and good service.

≫ For more exercises, go to **Practice file 9** on page 102.

8 Prepare a short presentation on how your company (or a company you know well) is competitive.
• Explain how you are competitive in your industry (e.g. price, choice).
• Explain what your company offers with words from **7**.
    Example: We offer good service.

9 Give your presentation to your partner or to the class.

Tip | Word stress
Note the different word stress:
com<u>pete</u>, com<u>pe</u>titive,
compe<u>ti</u>tion, com<u>pe</u>titor

Language at work | Comparatives

1 Do you normally buy these products or services from a shop/office or online from a website? Why? Compare your answers with the rest of the class.

- Music
- Food and drink
- Holidays or travel tickets
- Financial advice and loans
- Clothes
- Electrical goods
- Property (e.g. a house or flat)
- Books

2 Where does your company sell its products or services? In shops, over the Internet or somewhere else?

3 ▶ 9.2 Listen to two interviews with two business owners and answer the questions.

- Which speaker has an online retail/e-commerce company?
- Which speaker has a high street shop?

4 ▶ 9.2 The two speakers describe the competitive advantages of their companies. Listen again and complete the table.

Company 1	Company 2
a [1]_____ service	[5]_____ prices
staff are [2]_____ _____	[6]_____ stocks
staff are [3]_____	[7]_____ delivery
products are [4]_____ _____	a [8]_____ choice

5 Complete the *Language point* table for comparative adjectives. Use audio script 9.2 to help you.

LANGUAGE POINT

Adjective	Comparative form	Examples
short adjectives (one-syllable)	add _____	*fast___, cheap___*
adjectives ending in -y	replace the -y with ___	*friendly* → _____, *easy* → _____
long adjectives (two/three/four/five syllables)	put _____ or *less* before the adjective	_____ *experienced*, *less expensive*
irregular adjectives	various forms	*bad* → *worse* *good* → _____

>> For more information, go to **Grammar reference** on page 103.

6 Complete this text with the comparative forms of the adjectives in brackets.

WHAT IS MULTICHANNEL SELLING?

Many people choose to shop online because they find it [1]*__easier__* (easy) than going to the high street. Retail websites often have a [2]_____ (wide) selection of products and [3]_____ (cheap) prices than in the shops. But some people think the service in shops is [4]_____ (friendly), and they believe the staff are [5]_____ (experienced) and give them [6]_____ (good) advice than an online shop. That's why successful modern companies sell their products both in shops and online: multichannel selling.

>> For more exercises, go to **Practice file 9** on page 103.

Tip | *than*

Remember to use *than* (not *like*) after comparative adjectives when comparing two things:

*Our products are cheaper **than** our competitor's.*

NOT ~~Our products are cheaper like our competitor's.~~

7 Work in groups of three. Make sentences from the words in the table below. **Student A** begins the sentence with any word from A. **Student B** continues the sentence. **Student C** finishes the sentence. Change roles after each sentence.

> *Example:* A *Supermarkets …*
> B *… have a wider choice*
> C *… than small shops.*

A	B		C
Coffee	wide choice		managers
English	difficult/easy to learn		sending an email
Cycling	up-to-date		Japanese
Tablets	big/small	than …	small shops
Directors	expensive/cheap		water
Sending a tweet	fast/slow		driving
Supermarkets	low/high prices		laptops
	experienced		

8 Work with a partner. Take turns to compare your company with a competitor or another company you know well. Compare things like:

- price
- customer service
- quality
- choice
- staff
- delivery

> *Example: My company's products are more expensive than our competitor's, but we offer a higher quality service.*

Practically speaking | How to say prices

1 Write these currencies next to the correct country 1–6.

euros (€) x2   dollars ($)   yuan (¥)   pounds (£)   yen (¥)

1 Spain _____   4 China _____
2 Japan _____   5 Germany _____
3 the UK _____   6 the USA _____

2 ▶ 9.3 Listen to three short conversations and tick (✓) the prices you hear.

¥2,860 ☐	$26.80 ☐	$500 ☐
$50 ☐	$28.60 ☐	€17.50 ☐
€29.99 ☐	¥2,690 ☐	$7.50 ☐
¥170 ☐	¥2,960 ☐	€11.79 ☐
€11.75 ☐	$7.15 ☐	$30 ☐

3 Work with a partner. Practise saying all the prices in **2**.

4 ▶ 9.3 Listen again and complete the information in 1–3.
1 Price of phone: _____
   Price of calls per month: _____ for ten hours; _____ for five hours
2 Delivery free on orders of more than _____
   Delivery per item: _____; Delivery for four items: _____
3 Normal price: _____; Discount with customer card: _____
   Final price: _____

5 Work with a partner. How much do these things cost in your town or city?
- a TV
- a pizza
- a bus or train ticket
- a smartphone
- a mid-range hotel

6 Talk about the prices of the things in **5** in the cities below. Do you think they are cheaper or more expensive than in your town or city?
- London
- Beijing
- New York
- Rome
- Tokyo

Business communication | Comparing and choosing

1 ▶9.4 Javier Sampedro works for a chain of shops. His company wants to update its website and sell products online. Javier asked two web design companies, Weblines and ITE, for quotes. He compares the quotes for his managing director at their weekly meeting. Listen to the meeting and complete the table. Tick (✓) the correct column.

	Weblines	ITE
Lower prices?		✓
Smaller company?		
Older company?		
Better quality of work?		
More experience with online businesses?		
Faster delivery?		

2 ▶9.4 Listen again and complete these sentences.

a How do they _____?

b ITE is _____.

c Are they _____?

d The quality is _____.

e The _____ of ITE is the two people have experience in the online marketing and sales industry.

f The _____ of Weblines is they don't usually work with online businesses.

g There's no _____.

h I _____ ITE.

i Let's _____ them.

3 Put a–i in **2** into categories 1–4.

1 Asking about differences: _a_ , ___

2 Talking about similarities: ___ , ___

3 Talking about differences: ___ , ___ , ___

4 Choosing: ___ , ___

4 Work with a partner.

Student A: Ask Student B about situations 1–3.

1 Transportation for work: a motorbike or a bicycle?

2 Employ a new person for your department: put an advert in a newspaper or use a recruitment agency?

3 English lessons: in a classroom with a teacher or online?

Student B: Talk about the similarities and differences.

Example: **A** *I want a motorbike or a bicycle for work. How do they compare?*
B *A bicycle is cheaper, but …*

5 Now change roles and discuss three more situations.

• Food for a conference: local or foreign dishes?

• A two-day training course: at work during the week or in a five-star hotel at the weekend?

• A holiday this summer: at home or abroad?

≫ For more exercises, go to **Practice file 9** on page 102.

6 Work with a partner. Discuss some quotes for a courier and a hotel. **Student A, turn to page 114. Student B, turn to page 117.**

Key expressions

Asking about differences
What's the difference?
How do they compare?
Are they better?

Talking about similarities
X does …, but Y also …
There's no difference.
… is similar (to …).

Talking about differences
They're (cheap)er / more …
The advantage of … is …
The disadvantage is …

Choosing
Let's choose …
This one's better.
I prefer …

Supermarket competition

I like Lidl because it's smaller than my old supermarket, so I can do my shopping much faster. There's a smaller range of products, but I can buy everything I want.

I like the fact that Aldi sells a lot of local products: British meat, milk, cheese and fruit and vegetables.

It's easy – at my old supermarket, my weekly shop was about £80; at Lidl it's only about £60!

I like the products in Aldi: good quality meat and cheese, and excellent German chocolate!

Discussion

1 Read customers' comments about Aldi and Lidl. Why do they shop there?

2 ▶ 9.5 Listen to an interview about the success of Aldi and Lidl. Which of the reasons in the comments in 1 are mentioned?

3 What areas do you think are important for supermarkets to be competitive?

4 Which foreign stores (e.g. supermarkets, clothes shops, restaurants) are successful in your country? Why?

Task

1 Work in groups of three. You want to set up a new supermarket in your country. You need to compete with the supermarkets which are there now. How can you make your supermarket competitive? Discuss the profile of the supermarkets in your country – is there a gap in the market? Decide on your new supermarket's:

• products: range, quality, prices, brands, suppliers

• stores: location, size and design

• service: customer service and other services you can offer

• marketing: how will you advertise? What message will you give to the customers?

2 Present your ideas to the class. Which group's supermarket is the most competitive?

Viewpoint 3 | Processes

Focus

1 Work with a partner. Which of the processes 1–5 do you do in your job? Which of the adjectives below do you think describes each process?

fast   slow   difficult   simple   long   short

1 Taking customer orders
2 Recruiting a new employee
3 Arranging team meetings
4 Booking travel arrangements
5 A manufacturing process

2 ▶01 Watch three people talking about some of the processes in 1. Answer the questions in the table.

	Speaker 1	Speaker 2	Speaker 3
Which process are they talking about?			
How do they describe the process?			

3 Compare your answers in **2** with a partner.

The ordering process

4 Work with a partner. Discuss how food companies deliver fresh food to shops, restaurants and hotels. Think of all the stages in the delivery process and make a list. Begin with: *The customer places the order.*

5 Work with another pair of students in groups of four. Compare your lists of stages. Are there any differences?

The Fresh Direct ordering process

6 You are going to watch a video about the ordering process at a food delivery company. Before you watch, match words 1–10 from the video to definitions a–j.

1 supply chain ___
2 restaurant chains ___
3 system ___
4 scan ___
5 in stock ___
6 key into ___
7 allocate ___
8 assemble ___
9 pallet ___
10 picker ___

a type information into a computer
b a set of things working together
c goods in your warehouse which are ready to sell
d a square wooden object for storing and transporting an order
e the stages in moving an order from the supplier to the customer
f give someone a job to do
g many restaurants in different places, owned by one company
h employee who picks the foods for an order
i check something electronically
j put different parts in one place

James Cartwright
Operations Manager, Fresh Direct

7 ▶02 James Cartwright is the Operations Manager for the food delivery company Fresh Direct. Watch the video and answer questions 1–3.
1 What kind of food does Fresh Direct supply?
2 Which part of Fresh Direct is the video about?
3 Why is Fresh Direct a successful company?

8 Work with a partner. Number the stages in the process at Fresh Direct in the correct order 1–7.
A 'picker' assembles the order onto a pallet. ___
They key the order into the management system. ___
Fresh Direct takes an order from a customer. ___
Another person checks the quantity and quality of the product. ___
The order management system knows if the order is in stock. ___
Lorries deliver it to the customers in different parts of the country. ___
They load the pallet onto the lorry. ___

9 ▶02 Watch the video again and check your answers in **8**.

10 Work with a partner. Have a conversation using the information in **7** and **8**.
Student A: You are the operations manager at Fresh Direct. Welcome Student B to your warehouse and explain the process.
Student B: You are an important customer of Fresh Direct. You are visiting the warehouse for the first time. Ask Student A questions about the process in the warehouse.

Describe a process

11 Work with a partner. Think of a process you and/or your partner has at work. Make notes on all the stages of the process. Ask each other questions to help make each step of the process clear. Then present your process to the class.

10 Teamwork

Starting point

1 Do you usually work alone or in a team?

2 What are the advantages of working in a team?

3 When you make decisions, do you always ask for other opinions?

4 Do you have your best ideas on your own or with others?

Working with words | Working in teams

1 Read about W.L. Gore & Associates. Write the headings from the list in the correct place in the text 1–4.

Time to talk   Small teams   Everyone's a leader   The long view

Who's my BOSS?

W.L. Gore & Associates is well known for its GORE-TEX® fabrics. Wilbert and Genevieve Gore started the company in 1958. It has no bosses or job titles. The company's rules for business are:

1 _____
You work with colleagues in groups and everyone knows each other.

2 _____
There are no job titles and no managers, so everyone in the group makes decisions. You develop ideas to share with your team, and you all plan new projects together.

3 _____
It often takes years to solve problems and find solutions for new products.

4 _____
You attend lots of meetings. Face-to-face communication is better than memos and emails.

GUARANTEED TO KEEP YOU DRY
GORE-TEX® PRODUCTS
GORE PRO

2 Tick (✓) the phrases you think people say at Gore.
 1 I don't like working with other people. ☐
 2 I don't know – ask the boss. ☐
 3 Let's have a meeting. ☐
 4 It took a long time, but we have a great product. ☐
 5 It's not my job to think of new ideas. ☐
 6 I need to speak to the team before I make a decision. ☐

3 Work with a partner. Discuss which of Gore's working methods are similar in your company.

4 Match verbs 1–7 to nouns a–g, then check your answers in the text in **1**.
 1 attend ___   a decisions
 2 plan ___   b problems
 3 make ___   c solutions
 4 work ___   d projects
 5 develop ___   e meetings
 6 find ___   f with colleagues
 7 solve ___   g ideas

5 Complete these questions with words from **4**.
 1 What _____ do you have to make at work?
 2 What meetings did you _____ last month?
 3 Do you _____ with colleagues in a team, or alone?
 4 What do you do when you want to _____ a problem at work?
 5 What is a good time of day to _____ new ideas?
 6 How do you feel when you find a _____ to a problem?
 7 Do you have to _____ any large projects in your team?

6 Work with a partner. Ask and answer the questions in **5**.

7 ▶ 10.1 Listen to a conversation about a team problem. What is the problem? What three solutions do they talk about?

8 ▶ 10.1 Listen again and complete the sentences.
 1 I have a _____ problem with the new project team.
 2 There's a _____ problem with their teamwork …
 3 That's a _____ problem.
 4 That's a _____ idea!
 5 That might not be a _____ solution.
 6 I don't think that's such a _____ idea.

 ≫ For more exercises, go to **Practice file 10** on page 104.

9 Work with a partner. Discuss these problems using the phrases in **4** and **8**.
 • An important customer wants a 20% discount on all orders. You normally offer 10%.
 • Someone in your team is off sick for two weeks. You need to finish your project this Friday.
 • You have to take a new client to dinner. You need to decide where to go.
 • Two people in your team are good at their jobs, but there is a personality problem: they cannot work together and always disagree in meetings.

10 Think of a problem you have, or had, at work. Tell your partner and discuss it. Can you solve the problem?

Tip | *team*

A *team* is a group of people. We can use it as a singular or plural noun:
*The new **team is** planning the project.*
*The new **team are** planning the project.*

Language at work | Superlatives

Richard *Production Manager, Head office, Rio de Janeiro*

1 ▶ 10.2 Richard, Adriana and Pedro all work for an industrial supplies company in Brazil. Adriana is visiting the factory in Recife. She calls her colleague, Richard, in head office to report back. Listen to the phone call. Which problems do they talk about: technical, personnel or supply?

2 ▶ 10.2 Listen again. Are these sentences true (*T*) or false (*F*)?
1 The problem at the Recife factory is *small*. ___
2 The new components were *the most expensive* solution. ___
3 The new components were *the best* idea. ___
4 Pedro thinks the new components are *better* than the old ones. ___
5 Personnel problems at the factory are *bigger* than technical problems. ___
6 Staff turnover in the Recife factory is *the highest* of all the factories. ___
7 The team at the Recife factory is *the biggest* problem. ___

3 Which sentences in **2** ...?
a compare two or more things ___, ___
b say something is the maximum or minimum ___, ___, ___, ___

4 The sentences in **3b** use the superlative form. Complete the *Language point* table for superlatives. Use audio script 10.2 to help you.

Adriana *Technical Manager, Head office, Rio de Janeiro*

Pedro *Line Manager, Recife factory*

LANGUAGE POINT

Adjective	Superlative form	Examples
short adjectives, e.g. *small*	add _____	*the small* _____
	For adjectives ending in -*e*, add -*st*.	*the late* _____
	For adjectives ending in vowel + consonant, double the consonant and add + -*est*.	*the big* _____
adjectives ending in -*y*, e.g. *easy*	replace -*y* with _____ and add -*est*	*friendly* → *the* _____, *easy* → *the* _____
long adjectives, e.g. *expensive*	put _____ or *least* before the adjective	*the* _____ *expensive*, *the least expensive*
irregular adjectives, e.g. *good*	*the* + various forms	*bad* → *the worst* *good* → _____

>> For more information, go to **Grammar reference** on page 105.

5 Three days later, Richard and Adriana email each other. Complete their emails with the superlative form of the adjectives in brackets.

✉

Hi Adriana,

How was your trip? We have a lot of things to discuss, but ¹_____ (important) decision at the moment is what to do with Pedro. Should we ask him to leave, offer him a different job in Recife or move him to Rio? What's ²_____ (good) solution? Perhaps ³_____ (cheap) solution is to offer Pedro a new job in the Recife factory. What do you think?

Richard

✉

Hi Richard,

My trip was fine, except for this personnel problem.

Asking Pedro to leave is probably ⁴_____ (easy), but also ⁵_____ (expensive) solution. Sorry, but I think that offering him a new job in the Recife factory is ⁶_____ (bad) solution. You're right that it's ⁷_____ (expensive) option, but Recife is our ⁸_____ (small) factory, so he will still be dealing with the same people. How about transferring him to the new Rio factory? Let's talk about this when I'm back in the office.

Adriana

Tip | *personnel/personal*

Personnel is a noun and means staff or employees.
Personal is an adjective and means private or belonging to one person.
*Our **personnel** mustn't use their **personal** email addresses at work.*

6 Work with a partner. You need to find a new line manager for the Recife factory. Discuss and compare the three candidates below. Who is the best candidate?

Marcio	Paolo	Lucy
Rio de Janeiro factory	Recife factory	Recife factory
Work history		
• Joined the company in 2008 as a line worker. • Became team leader for Production line 1 in 2011.	• Joined the company as line worker last year. • Became team leader for Production line 2 this year.	• Joined the Denver factory in 2006. • Became team leader in 2012. Moved to Recife six months ago.
Comments		
Very popular with his team. He is looking for jobs in other companies.	Next month – training course in management skills.	Her team like her. She is taking Portuguese lessons.

>> For more exercises, go to **Practice file 10** on page 105.

7 Think of two or three answers for the following. Then tell your partner and compare them. Use the superlatives in brackets.
- Current problems you are having at work (smallest? biggest?)
- New products in your home or at work (newest? most expensive?)
- New ideas you had this week (worst? best?)
  Example: *I have a few problems at work … but the biggest problem I have is …*

Practically speaking | How to respond to news

1 ▶ 10.3 Which expressions a–f can you use to respond to the sentences 1–6? Listen and check your ideas.
1 I got a promotion to section manager.
2 I didn't get that sales job that I applied for.
3 I left my phone on the train.
4 Our boss got a new job with our biggest competitor.
5 Our company won retailer of the year.
6 We won the contract for the new shopping centre.

a Oh no. That's terrible.
b Really? How amazing!
c Great. That's fantastic!
d Wow. That is surprising.
e I'm sorry. How disappointing.
f Good. That's excellent news!

2 Put the expressions a–f in **1** into categories 1–3.
1 Responding to good news: ___, ___
2 Responding to bad news: ___, ___
3 Showing surprise: ___, ___

3 ▶ 10.3 Listen again and underline the stressed words and syllables in the expressions a–f in **1**. Then practise the conversations with a partner.

4 Work with a partner. **Student A**, turn to **page 114**. **Student B**, turn to **page 110**. Respond to each other's news.

Business communication | Giving opinions

1 Papotech, an office supply company, is currently having two problems: staff are leaving and customers are complaining. The Director at Papotech asked for this report. It compares his company with some competitors. Work in groups. Read the report and discuss possible reasons for the problems.

Example: Staff probably leave because Papotech pays the lowest salaries.

CONFIDENTIAL REPORT Comparison of Papotech and its competitors

	PAY	PRICES	CALL CENTRE	
	Average salary per month	Average price of popular products	Number of staff per 1,000 customers	Average call time
Papotech	€1,420	€325	1.2	3 mins 45 secs
Office First	€1,830	€317	1.7	2 mins 30 secs
TMP	€1,560	€284	1.8	3 mins 10 secs

2 ▶ 10.4 The Director is discussing the report with a line manager. Listen and answer questions 1–2.

1 Which parts of the report do they discuss? What don't they discuss?
2 What reasons does the line manager give for the two problems?

3 ▶ 10.4 Listen again. Put expressions a–h into categories 1–4.

1 Asking for an opinion: ___, ___   3 Agreeing: ___
2 Giving an opinion: ___, ___, ___   4 Disagreeing: ___, ___

a What's your opinion?   e Do you think …
b In my opinion …   f I don't think so.
c I think …   g I'm not so sure.
d I agree.   h I think we should …

>> For more exercises, go to **Practice file 10** on page 104.

4 Work with a partner. Discuss 1–4 below. Follow this model.

Ask B's opinion. → *Give your opinion.* → *Agree or disagree.*

1 Teams are always better than people working alone.
2 Meetings are never useful.
3 The best offer is usually the cheapest.
4 Employees prefer more pay than more training.

5 Work in small groups. Look at the ideas in the table. Discuss what you should do to solve the problems at Papotech. You have a maximum budget of €200,000.

PAPOTECH	Possible solutions	Cost in €
Prices	Offer 10% lower prices on 100 most popular products	
	a) to all customers	100,000
	b) to our biggest customers	45,000
Pay	Increase salaries	
	a) by 10%	50,000
	b) by 5%	25,000
Training	Give more training to call centre staff	10,000
Jobs	a) Recruit two new staff for the call centre	60,000
	b) Offer three staff the post of team leader	20,000
IT	a) Buy a new computer system	100,000
	b) Train staff to use the new system	15,000

Key expressions

Asking for an opinion
What do you think?
What's your opinion?
Do you think …?

Giving an opinion
In my opinion …
I think … / I don't think …
I think we should …

Agreeing
Yes, I agree.
That's true.

Disagreeing
I disagree / don't agree.
I'm not so sure.

Teamwork and personality types

What makes a good team? Some companies use tests to help them choose the right people to work together and to improve teamwork. The MBTI® (Myers-Briggs Type Indicator) is one of the most popular. It is used by 89 of the biggest companies in the USA.

In the MBTI® employees answer a lot of questions in four different categories. The result of the test tells employees that they have one of 16 different personality types. In this way, employers hope that employees will understand themselves and their colleagues better.

Case study: Kaiser Permanente, a large health-care provider in the USA.

Situation: A large administrative team working in two different offices in Northern and Southern California didn't work well as a team. Communication wasn't good and employees were stressed. They didn't agree on how to do things.

Action: Team-building training which used the MBTI® test.

Results: The team understood themselves and each other better. They organized their tasks differently, so their work became more efficient and they felt less stressed. 'It became much easier to understand why others act and communicate the way they do,' said one member of the team.

Discussion

1 Do you think using tests like the MBTI® is useful for companies? Why/Why not?

2 Are personality tests used by companies in your country? Does your company use them?

3 In what other ways do companies try to improve teamwork?

4 How does your company try to improve teamwork?

Task

1 Work with a partner. Ask and answer the questions.

Are you a team player?

1 **Do you prefer ...?**
   a to work in your own office   **b** to work in a shared office

2 **When you have a big problem at work, do you ...?**
   a usually discuss it with your colleagues   **b** prefer to think about it alone

3 **Do you prefer ...?**
   a to play a team sport, like football   **b** to exercise alone, like running

4 **When your colleagues have a question or problem, do they ...?**
   a often ask you for help   **b** usually ask other people for help

5 **At work, is it most important for you to ...?**
   a do work that gets results   **b** work with people you like

6 **Imagine your company has a team-building weekend. Do you think ...?**
   a 'Great! More fun with my colleagues!'   **b** 'Oh no! Another team-building event!'

2 With your partner, discuss what you think your answers say about your personality type. How is this important for your work in a team?

11 Travel

Starting point

1 Do you often travel on business/holiday?

2 What is your favourite destination? Why?

3 How do you travel?

Working with words | Staying at a hotel

1 When was the last time you stayed in a hotel? Was it a work or leisure trip? Which of these facilities and services did the hotel have?

restaurant   gym   car park   Internet access
swimming pool   room service   other services

2 ▶11.1 Jenny Chiang is on a business trip to Dublin. She needs to book a hotel room. Listen to her phone conversation with the receptionist and choose the correct words from 1–5 on the reservation form.

RESERVATION FORM

Name   Jenny Chiang

Date   24th October

Room type   ¹*single / double*

Price   €120 (bed and breakfast)

²*Credit card / Passport* details   ³*Mastercard / Visa*

⁴*Phone / Card* number   6674 8596 8374 6374

⁵*Expiry / Start* date   03/2019

---

3 ▶11.1 Match 1–5 to a–e to make phrases from the conversation. Then listen again and check.

1 I'd like to book ___   a the terminal.
2 Do you have ___   b breakfast?
3 Does that include ___   c any vacancies?
4 You can check in ___   d a room for the night.
5 There's a free bus from ___   e anytime now.

4 ▶11.2 Now listen to Jenny's conversation when she arrives at the hotel. Answer questions 1–3.

1 What is Jenny's room number?
2 What time can she have breakfast?
3 Does she need to make a reservation for dinner?

5 ▶11.2 Listen again and complete these phrases from the conversation.

1 I have a _____ for tonight.
2 Your room is on the fifth _____.
3 The _____ is over there.
4 What time is breakfast _____?
5 Do I need to _____ a table?

6 ▶ 11.3 Jenny calls Reception. Listen and tick (✓) the things she asks about.

towels ☐	a safe ☐
room service ☐	Internet access ☐
a taxi ☐	a wake-up call ☐
a hairdryer ☐	

7 Complete the sentences with the words from **6**.

1 Can I have _____ at 6 a.m. please?
2 Do I need a password for the _____ in my room?
3 Can you order _____ to the airport for me?
4 There is _____ on the wall in the bathroom.
5 Can I have some more _____ for my room, please?
6 Is there _____ in the room for valuables?
7 The restaurant closes at 10 p.m. but _____ is available until midnight.

>> For more exercises, go to **Practice file 11** on page 106.

8 Work with a partner.
Student A: You are a hotel receptionist at Metro Hotel. Look at the information below and answer questions about the services.
Student B: Turn to **page 118** and ask questions about the services.
Use the phrases in **3, 5** and **7** to help you.

METRO HOTEL

SERVICES

We are pleased to offer guests many services:

ROOM SERVICE (310)
Order food in your room from 07.00–00.00.

WAKE-UP CALL (311)
Phone for an early morning wake-up call.
We can also order taxis to the airport.

BREAKFAST (313)
Served in the restaurant from 07.00–09.30.
(Also available in rooms.)

RESTAURANT (313)
Book a table for dinner this evening at our French restaurant.

BUSINESS SERVICES (314)
One meeting room is available.
Please book in advance.

GYM AND SAUNA
On basement floor. Open 24 hours a day.

ALL ROOMS HAVE:
• wireless Internet access
• pay-per-view TV with eight film channels
• air conditioning

9 Change roles and repeat **8**. **Student A**, turn to **page 114** and ask questions about the services. Use the phrases in **3, 5** and **7** to help you.

Language at work | *Going to* | Infinitive of purpose

1 Read this article and answer questions 1–4.
  1 What problem do business travellers have?
  2 What service does the company offer?
  3 Where do they operate?
  4 What are their plans?

TOUR GUIDES ON THE RUN

On your next business trip, **are you going to have** any time for sightseeing? Probably not. Even when it's a famous destination, most business travellers **aren't going to see** outside the airport, hotel or conference room. But City Running Tours has the solution. Go for a run with a tour guide across the city and see all the local places of interest before breakfast. The company now offers tours of 12 US cities, from Atlanta to Washington DC, including Honolulu! And you can cross the border to Canada, too, for a tour of Toronto. It is now so popular with business travellers that **they're going to offer** the service in even more cities in the future.

2 Look at the phrases in **bold** in **1**. Are they about the past, present or future? Are they about a general plan or a specific arrangement?

3 Complete the explanations in *Language point 1* with *be*, *main verb* and *going to*.

LANGUAGE POINT 1

1 We talk about general plans with _____ + _____ + _____.
2 In negative sentences, we use the negative of _____.

>> For more information, go to **Grammar reference** on page 107.

4 Work with a partner. Take turns to ask and answer questions about Mike's plans for a business trip to Canada. Use the notes below.

  Example: **A** *Is he going to see Christophe?*
  B *No, he isn't, but he's going to meet Dominic.*

> * have dinner with colleagues ✓
> * see Christophe ✗ (meet Dominic)
> * present new product ✓
> * open new sales office ✓
> * visit Ottawa office ✗ (visit Montreal)
> * take train to Montreal ✓
> * go sightseeing ✗ (no time)

5 Work with a partner. Ask and answer questions about your next trip or holiday.

		visit …
		open …
Are you		have …
I'm	going to	see …
We're		offer …
		take …
		meet …

6 ▶11.4 Listen to a conversation with a business traveller. Where is he going?

7 ▶11.4 Listen again and match 1–4 to a–d.
1 I'm going to visit Toronto first ___
2 I'm going to spend a day in Quebec ___
3 We're going out in the evening ___
4 I'm going to take Friday off ___

a **to present** the new product to Dominic and his team.
b **to see** the old city and have dinner.
c **to see** the sales reps there.
d **to have** a nice long weekend.

8 Answer the questions in *Language point 2*.

> **LANGUAGE POINT 2**
>
> What form are the verbs in **bold** in **7**?
> Is this form used here to say …?
>   1 why something happens
>   2 how something happens
>   3 when something happens

9 Work with a partner. Make sentences about plans using the prompts.
1 leave work early → go to the dentist
2 do a course → learn a new computer program
3 visit Delhi → see clients
4 call Sashia → arrange a meeting
5 come to the office at the weekend → finish my report

> *Example: I'm going to leave work early to go to the dentist.*

>> For more exercises, go to **Practice file 11** on page 107.

10 Write three plans for you or your company. Tell your partner about them.

Practically speaking | How to talk about money

1 ▶11.5 Listen to three conversations about money and match them to places a–c.
a bureau de change ___
b taxi ___
c airport shop ___

2 ▶11.5 How much money does the traveller pay or get in each conversation?

3 ▶11.5 Listen again and complete these sentences.
1 How _____ is that?
2 Keep the _____.
3 Can I pay _____ credit card?
4 I'd like to _____ $500 …
5 The exchange _____ is …
6 What's the _____?

4 Work with a partner. Role-play the three situations in the pictures.

Business communication | Eating out

1 Work with a partner. Read this article and discuss the questions for:
1 your own country
2 other countries you visit

Tips for travellers

Eating out

In many countries, the restaurant – not the office – is the real place for business. So make sure you can answer these questions before your next trip abroad.

1 What do you eat for lunch or dinner?
2 Are there any special or local dishes?
3 What are the most popular drinks with dinner?
4 How many courses are there?
5 Who pays the bill?
6 What is the tip in restaurants? 0%? 10%? 20%?

2 ▶ 11.6 Listen to two people at an airport restaurant ordering from the menu below. What do they order? What is their total bill?

★ **FLYING HIGH** ★
MENU

Chicken salad **8.95**

Spaghetti Bolognese **11.25**

Fish pie **11.25**

Steak and fries **13.50**

Vegetable risotto **8.50**

Giant burger and fries **11.25**

Pizza: tomato and mozarella / pepperoni / chicken and mushroom **10.50**

Side dishes: mixed salad / french fries / grilled vegetables **4.95**

Bottled water (sparkling or still) **4.50**

Soft drinks / coffee / tea **3.00**

---

3 ▶ 11.6 Listen again and <u>underline</u> the correct words in *italics*.
1 *Would / Do* you like pizza?
2 *Do / Are* you ready to order?
3 *Do you like / Would you like* to order first?
4 *I'd / I'll* have the vegetable risotto, please.
5 *I like / I'd like* the pepperoni pizza, please.
6 *What / How* was your meal?
7 *Would you like / Do you like* a dessert?
8 *I'll just have / I just like* a coffee.
9 *We'll / We'd* like two coffees, please.
10 *Could / Would* I have the bill, please?

4 Which of the expressions in *italics* mean (*a*) *Do you want ...?*, (*b*) *I/We want ...* or (*c*) neither?
1 *Do you like* pizza? ___
2 *Are you ready* to order? ___
3 *We like* sparkling water. ___
4 *We'd like* sparkling water. ___
5 *Do you have* pizza? ___
6 *I'll have* the pepperoni pizza. ___
7 *Would you like* a dessert? ___
8 *Could I have* the bill? ___

>> For more exercises, go to **Practice file 11** on page 106.

5 Work in groups of three. Take turns to be customers and a waiter at the airport restaurant. Use the menu in **2** and practise ordering food and talking about the food with your partner. Use the expressions in **3** to help you.

Key expressions

Offering
Would you like ...?

Asking for information
Are you ready to order?
Do you have (any) ...?

Requesting
Could I have ...?
I'd like ..., please.
I'll have ..., please.

Responding
Yes, please.
No, thanks.
Not for me, thanks.
Sure.
Of course.

Talking about food
Do you like ...?
They have really good ... here.
How was your meal?
Delicious / Very nice.
The pizza looks/sounds good.

TALKING POINT

More efficient business trips

Business trips are important for many companies, but even a short trip can cost a lot: travel, hotels, food – and time! How can you get the most for your time and money?

- Book flights early. They are usually cheaper then.
- Use a business travel agent to save time and get better prices.
- Is there another way to travel? Train tickets are often cheaper than flights, and an overnight train journey can replace a night in a hotel. If the journey isn't too long, some employees like to drive so that they can choose when to go.
- Are you going to network at a conference or trade fair? Use social media to connect with other people before you arrive.
- Do you have friends or family you can stay with? Or how about Airbnb, where you rent a room or apartment directly from the owner? 1,000 companies already use Airbnb for employees on business trips.
- Meet people for coffee, not dinner, and you will have time for more meetings.
- Use public transport and/or the airport shuttle bus instead of taxis.
- Do you really need to go? Can you hold the meeting by teleconference or videoconference instead?

Discussion

1 Do you agree or disagree with each of the ideas above?

2 How do you travel? How can you reduce the time and money you spend on travelling?

3 Do you think people go on fewer business trips these days because of tele- and videoconferencing? How do you think business travel will change in the future?

Task

1 Work in small groups. Look at the travel and meetings plan for a sales manager in a Madrid-based company. Use the travel and accommodation information on **page 115** to help plan the manager's trips. Discuss the options, for example:

- Can some meetings take place using videoconferencing instead of a personal meeting?

- How will they travel? Where will they stay?

- Are there any ways to save time and money?

Sales Department Travel and meetings			
March	MEETING	LOCATION	TIME
21st	First meeting with a possible customer	Lisbon	10 a.m.
23rd–24th	European sales and marketing meeting	Paris	two full days
25th	Meeting with an important customer	Lisbon	to be confirmed
26th	Hospitality trade fair	Lyon	all day
before the end of the month	New product training for team (The team come from Barcelona, Bilbao, Lisbon and Malaga. They usually travel by car [4–6 hours] or can fly [1 hour, 25 minutes].)	Madrid	half day

12 Schedules

Starting point

1 What's your busiest month?

2 Which month do you normally take a holiday in?

3 Which is your favourite season: spring, summer, autumn or winter? Why?

Working with words | Calendars and schedules

1 Work with a partner. What do you think the busiest season is for these types of business? Why?

- delivering flowers
- department store
- trade fair industry

2 The graphs below show busy periods in the year for the three businesses in **1**. Match the graphs A–C to the three businesses.

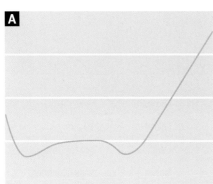

J F M A M J J A S O N D

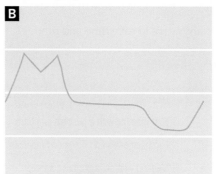

J F M A M J J A S O N D

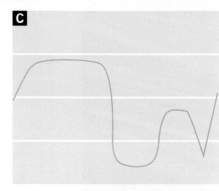

J F M A M J J A S O N D

3 ▶ 12.1 Listen to three people who work in these businesses. Check your answers in **2** and answer questions 1–3.

1 Which months are busiest for Katrina?

2 Why is January a good month for department stores?

3 Which days are very important in the flower delivery business?

Tip | *schedule*

Schedule is pronounced differently in British English and American English:
British English: /'ʃedjuːl/
American English: /'skedʒuːl/

4 Complete word pairs 1–7 with words from the list. Use audio script 12.1 to help you.

holiday   period (x2)   off   schedule   deadline   leave

1 tight _____
2 busy _____
3 annual _____
4 public _____

5 busy _____
6 quiet _____
7 time _____

5 Complete these questions with words from **4**.

1 Do you have a busy _____ and a _____ period during the day?
2 Do have any time _____ this month? When is your annual _____?
3 Many companies have _____ deadlines around Christmas. Is this true for your company?
4 What happens if a _____ holiday is at the weekend?

6 Work with a partner. Ask and answer the questions in **5**.

7 Look at the schedule and note below. Whose schedule is this from **3**? Are they busy all week?

Wednesday 27th	Final day for annual conference registrations
	8 p.m. Dinner with Franco at Nara Sushi at Friesenstrasse 70
Thursday 28th	10 a.m. Open trade fair stand
	2 p.m. Meet association members
Friday 29th	Day off – Long weekend in Paris!

Don't forget!

1 Email this timetable to Franco.

2 Email a reminder to members about Thursday meeting.

8 Find four words or phrases in the schedule and note in **7** for definitions 1–4.

1 time off on Saturday, Sunday and one extra day (Friday or Monday) _____
2 a note to tell you to do something _____
3 a plan or schedule with times for each stage _____
4 meeting for a group of people once a year _____

» For more exercises, go to **Practice file 12** on page 108.

9 Which are the busy periods in your company? Draw a line in the graph below to show your busier and quieter months. Work with a partner. Use your graph to talk about the following:

- the busier and quieter seasons
- time off and holidays this year
- deadlines this month
- your schedule or timetable this week
- events you have every year

  Example: I have a very busy schedule this month because …

J F M A M J J A S O N D

Language at work | Present perfect

1 Greta Helsing works for Original Oils. Read the information about the company and her email below and answer questions 1–3.

1 Where does Original Oils sell its products?
2 Where does it buy its materials?
3 What is Greta's deadline?

Original Oils

Original Oils imports and sells natural cosmetic products (soap, lotions) to high street shops in Western Europe. Usually, the company buys raw materials from Pakistan and India, but this year Original Oils **has ordered** Palmarosa oil from a new supplier in Nepal. It wants to produce a new soap with the oil for Valentine's Day but the delivery **hasn't arrived yet**.

✉

Subject: Palmarosa soap

Dear Barati,

How are you? Can you update us on our order? I have checked our system, but it hasn't arrived yet. **Have you shipped** the oil yet? We need the delivery by 20th October.

Greta Helsing
Original Oils

---

2 Answer the questions in the *Language point*.

> **LANGUAGE POINT**
>
> Look at the verbs in **bold** in **1**.
> 1 Are they talking/asking about a past, present or future action?
> 2 Does the action affect the present or the past?
>
> Complete these explanations for forming the present perfect.
> a To make positive statements use *have*/_____ + past participle.
> b To make negative sentences use *haven't*/_____ + past participle.
> c To make questions use _____/_____ + subject + past participle.
> d To form the past participle of regular verbs (*order*, *arrive*, etc.) add _____ to the verb.

» For more information, go to **Grammar reference** on page 109.

3 Work with a partner. Look at Barati's list. Take turns to ask what he has done.
   Example: **A** *Has he checked the database?*   **B** *Yes, he has.*

Check database ✓
Contact shipping firm ✓
Email producer ✓
Call Greta ✗
Arrange next visit to producers ✗
Update website with product details ✓

Tip | *yet*
With the negative and question forms of the present perfect, you can add *yet* to say that you intend to do it:
I haven't done it **yet** *(but I'm going to ...).*

4 ▶12.2 Listen to the phone call. Is the delivery going to be late? What is Greta going to change?

5 ▶12.2 Listen again and complete sentences 1–6 with the present perfect of the verbs in brackets.
1 We _____ (send) it …
2 We _____ (have) a few problems here.
3 _____ you _____ (take) lots of orders for the soap?
4 There _____ (be) a lot of interest.
5 _____ you _____ (see) some of the other products on our website?
6 _____ you ever _____ (be) to Nepal?

6 Read the final part of audio script 12.2 on **page 126**. How does Greta give short answers in the present perfect?

>> For more exercises, go to **Practice file 12** on page 109.

7 Work with a partner. You each have some tasks to complete before the end of the week. Ask each other about your progress on the tasks. **Student A**, turn to **page 115. Student B**, turn to **page 112.**

Practically speaking | How to use prepositions of time

1 ▶12.3 Listen to two people talking about their jobs. What industry do they work in? When are they busiest?

2 ▶12.3 Complete sentences 1–6 with the correct prepositions from the list. Then listen again and check.
on (x2)   *in* (x2)   *at* (x2)
1 My busiest period is _____ spring.
2 My flight is _____ ten.
3 The conference starts _____ the 13th.
4 What are you going to do _____ the weekend?
5 We are open _____ public holidays.
6 The restaurant is closed _____ May.

3 Put the prepositions from **2** into the table.

1 _____	2 _____	3 _____
… Monday	… February	… nine-thirty
… 21st of November	… winter	… midday
… New Year's Day	… spring	… the weekend
	… an hour	

4 Ask your partner about these times. Ask about the past, present and future.
• in spring/summer/autumn/winter
• in (month)
• at (time)
• at the weekend
• on public holidays
• on the (date)
   Example: What did you do at the weekend? What do you usually do on public holidays? What are you going to do in the summer?

Tip | at or on?
The prepositions *at* and *on* are sometimes used in different ways in British and American English:
British English: What are you going to do **at** *the weekend?*
American English: What are you going to do **on** *the weekend?*

81

Business communication | Planning a schedule

1 ▶ 12.4 Greta Helsing is meeting with Soledad and Martin at Original Oils. They are discussing and planning the schedule for the new Palmarosa Soap. Martin is coordinating production and Soledad deals with sales to the high street shops. Listen to the meeting. Complete Greta's notes with the dates.

Palmarosa Soap
Must be on the shelves by ¹_____
Launch date ²_____
Packaging ready by ³_____
Final product ready by ⁴_____
Start delivery to shops on ⁵_____

2 ▶ 12.4 Listen again and match 1–12 to a–l to make sentences.

1 … the schedule is ___	a taken it to the warehouse.
2 The situation is ___	b for this?
3 … we've already ___	c to launch it on January the 20th.
4 The aim is to ___	d deliver the product …?
5 What's the deadline ___	e get the soap on the shelves …
6 What date is ___	f with that date?
7 We plan ___	g do we need for production?
8 How much time ___	h about a week late.
9 Why don't we ___	i delivery from the warehouse …
10 Let's start ___	j going to call our packaging people …
11 Is everyone happy ___	k that the raw material from Nepal has just arrived.
12 So, to summarize, I'm ___	l the launch?

3 Put the sentences in **2** into categories 1–5.
1 Stating the current situation: ___, ___, ___
2 Saying what needs to be done: ___, ___
3 Asking about dates and times: ___, ___, ___
4 Proposing a plan: ___, ___
5 Summarizing and confirming the plan: ___, ___

❯❯ For more exercises, go to **Practice file 12** on page 108.

4 Work in groups of three. You are preparing a company brochure for next year. Today's date is 1st July. **Student A** turn to **page 115**. **Student B** turn to **page 113**. **Student C** turn to **page 112**.

5 Present your schedule to another group. How similar are your schedules?

6 Make a list of the stages in a typical schedule in your company.
Example: • *invoicing customers each month*
• *arranging the weekly staff meeting*
• *the stages for a new product*
• *arranging the annual conference*

7 Present the stages in **6** to the class and say how long each stage usually takes.

Key expressions

Stating the current situation
At the moment, the schedule …
The situation is that …
We've already …

Saying what needs to be done
The aim is to …
We plan to …

Asking about dates and times
What's the deadline?
What date …?
How much time do we need for …?

Proposing a plan
What if …?
Let's …
Why don't we …?

Summarizing/confirming the plan
Is everyone happy with that date?
I'm/You're/We're going to …
So, to summarize …

TALKING POINT

The revision game

Work with a partner. Take turns to choose a square.
- On a yellow square, have a role-play with your partner; on a blue square, follow the instruction; on a pink square, answer the question(s).
- If you are correct, or if you complete the role-play, you win the square.
- If you are not correct, the square stays open.
- The winner is the first person to win five squares in a row, across ➡, down ⬇ or diagonally ↘.

Question: Where are you from? What is your nationality? What is your job?	**Instruction:** Find the mistake: Are you from Peru? Yes, I from.	**Question:** When you check in to a hotel, what is the procedure?	**Instruction:** Explain how to use the photocopier.	**Instruction:** Talk about your last phone call. Who was it with? What was it about?
Role-play: A Call a hotel and ask about its services, then book a room. B Answer B's questions.	**Question:** Which words go together? tight / leave / annual / schedule / busy / deadline	**Role-play:** A Introduce yourself to B – you've never met. B Respond.	**Instruction:** Compare your company to its competitors.	**Question:** Can I join you? Do you come here often?
Instruction: Ask your partner three questions about his/her job.	**Role-play:** Give your opinion on this then ask for B's opinion: Your CEO wants to move your offices to a city 500 km away.	**Instruction:** Talk about your job and your responsibilities.	**Question:** What's your company working on at the moment?	**Role-play:** A You want to speak to a colleague but he/she isn't there. Leave a message. B Answer the call.
Role-play: A Call your partner and ask for his/her email address. B Respond.	**Question:** What have you done today?	**Question:** What is the location of your company and what is near it?	**Instruction:** Think of three qualities that these jobs need: airline pilot, administrator	**Question:** What do you do if you work in real estate?
Instruction: Describe your favourite restaurant using superlatives, e.g. best, most expensive, etc.	**Role-play:** Plan a party for your English group next week. Discuss with B your plan and the schedule.	**Instruction:** Describe a typical day at work. Use these words: always, often, rarely, sometimes, usually, and never	**Question:** Where is your head office? What other workplaces does your company have?	**Instruction:** Give a visitor to your company directions from Reception to your office.
Role-play: A Arrive at a hotel and check in. Ask about breakfast and dinner. B Respond.	**Instruction:** Talk about your last trip. Where did you go? How long did you stay? When did you leave/arrive?	**Question:** What are your plans for the next year / few months? Why are you doing this?	**Role-play:** A Call and arrange a meeting for next week. B Respond.	**Instruction:** Ask for help to print a document.

Focus

1 Work with a partner. Have you ever been on a business trip and had problems? Look at the list of problems. Have these ever happened to you? What did you do?
- You missed the plane.
- The plane was cancelled.
- Your bags didn't arrive at the airport.
- The hotel didn't have a room for you.
- A member of the hotel staff was rude.
- The food in the hotel restaurant was terrible.
- There was something wrong with your room.
- Something else?

DESTINATION	FLIGHT	GATE	REMAR
BERLIN	LH543	09	:DELA
NEW YORK	AA978	28	:CANC
TORONTO	AC902	11	:CANC
MADRID	IB342	15	:CANCE
BEIJING	CX654	02	:CANCE
HOUSTON	AA384	08	:CANCE
PARIS			

2 You are going to watch two videos about a business trip. One video is in a hotel reception and the other video is in a restaurant. Before you watch, look at sentences 1–12. Do you think the sentences are in a hotel reception (H) or in a restaurant (R)? Which can be in both places (H/R)?

1 I have a reservation. _H/R_
2 Are you ready to order now? ___
3 Would you like a wake-up call? ___
4 Table for two? ___
5 Can someone check the air conditioning? ___
6 What do you recommend? ___
7 Would you like help with your bags? ___
8 Do you need another moment with the menu? ___
9 Could you just sign here? ___
10 Do you need a taxi? ___
11 I'll get this. ___
12 If you could check the amount and enter your pin number please? ___

Checking into a hotel

3 ▶01 Patricia Reyes is a consultant in market research. She is on a business trip to do some work for a company in a different city. Watch Patricia Reyes checking into a hotel. Tick (✓) the phrases you hear in 2.

4 ▶01 Watch the video again. Are these statements true (T) or false (F)?
1 Patricia is staying for three nights. ___
2 Patricia is on the first floor in Room 115. ___
3 Breakfast is between 7.00 and 9.45. ___
4 She'd like a wake-up call at 7.00. ___
5 She doesn't need a newspaper. ___
6 She has a problem with the Internet password in the room. ___
7 She couldn't find the dial for the air conditioning. ___
8 The receptionist will order a taxi for her. ___

A business lunch

5 ▶02 Patricia meets one of her clients, Marcus, for lunch in a restaurant. Watch the video and tick (✓) the phrases you hear in **2**.

6 ▶02 Watch the video again. Answer questions 1–10.
1. Who gave the presentation in the morning?
2. Why is Marcus pleased with Patricia?
3. Do they both order sparkling water?
4. Do they order their food straightaway?
5. How long has Marcus worked for his company?
6. What do they order?
7. How is Patricia's hotel?
8. What is the problem with Marcus's order?
9. Who pays for the meal?
10. What is Patricia going to do later in the day?

Business trip problems

7 Work with a partner. Read problems 1–9. What can you say to the hotel receptionist or waiter in each situation?
1. You check into a hotel. You reserved a double room at the hotel but the receptionist only has a single room available.
2. Your bags are very heavy. You need help with them.
3. The TV in your hotel room isn't working.
4. The hotel room is cold and you don't know how to turn the heating on.
5. You booked a taxi with the hotel reception for 7.00 p.m. Now you are waiting in reception and it's 7.15 p.m.
6. Finally, you arrive at the restaurant and meet a friend. You sit down but no one gives you a menu.
7. You order your meal but the waiter brings you the wrong dish.
8. You ask for the bill. It has an extra $20 for wine but you didn't have any wine.
9. You want to pay by credit card but the restaurant doesn't take your type of card.

8 Practise the conversations in each situation in **7**.
Student A: You are the visitor. Explain each problem.
Student B: You are the hotel receptionist or the waiter. Try to solve Student A's problems.

9 Swap roles in **8** and repeat the conversations.

Working with words

1 Match products 1–8 to their nationalities a–h.

1 Coca Cola ___	a American
2 De Beer diamonds ___	b Indian
3 British Airways airline ___	c Japanese
4 Sanyo electronics ___	d British
5 LOT airline ___	e Polish
6 Andhra Rice ___	f Brazilian
7 Fiat cars ___	g South African
8 Cachaça rum ___	h Italian

2 Complete the job titles 1–6.

1 P__r__o__a__ A__s__s__a__t
2 S__l__s R__p
3 F__n__n__i__l D__r__c__o__
4 H__m__n R__s__u__c__s M__n__g__r
5 T__a__ L__a__e__
6 T__c__n__c__a__
7 R__c__p__i__n__s__

3 Read the business cards and complete each business person's profile.

Haruo Ogawa
Financial Director

TOYOTA JAPAN

I'm ¹_____ (name).
I'm from ²_____ (country)
and I'm a ³_____ (job).
My company is ⁴_____
(nationality).

Isadora De Souza
RECEPTIONIST

PETROBRAS
BRASIL

Her name is ⁵_____.
She's ⁶_____ (nationality).
She's a ⁷_____ (job).
Her company is in ⁸_____
(country).

JADE BOTHA • TEAM LEADER

SA Airlink
SOUTH AFRICA

I'm ⁹_____ (name).
I'm from ¹⁰_____ (country)
and I'm a ¹¹_____ (job).
My company is ¹²_____ (nationality).

Business communication

1 Put these conversations in the correct order.

1 a ___ I'm fine. This is my colleague, Martin Altenberg.
  b ___ Hello. Pleased to meet you, Gundula. How are you?
  c ___ How do you do, Martin?
  d ___ Hello. My name's Gundula Bauer.

2 a ___ No. How do you do? I'm Stefani.
  b ___ Do you know Ariadne?
  c ___ And you.
  d ___ Pleased to meet you, Stefani.

3 a ___ Thanks. Nice meeting you and your colleague.
  b ___ Bye.
  c ___ Yes, have a good journey.
  d ___ It's time to leave. See you soon.
  e ___ Goodbye.

2 Underline the correct words in *italics* to complete the three conversations.

A ¹*This is Pietre. / How are you?* He's my assistant.
B ²*How do you do? / Nice to meet you, too.* Pleased to meet you.
A ³*I'm fine. / And you.*

C ⁴*Do you know Franziska? / How do you do?*
D Yes! ⁵*I'm fine. / It's good to see you again.*
C Yes, you too. ⁶*Nice meeting you. / How are you?*
D I'm fine. And you?

E Good morning. I have an appointment with Ms Cernoskova. ⁷*This is / My name's* Ludmilla Osimk.
F ⁸*How do you do? / It's good to see you again.* I'm Timo, Ms Cernoskova's assistant.
E Oh, ⁹*nice to meet you. / have a good journey.*

3 Complete the conversation with the expressions from the list.

Nice meeting you   see you soon   How do you do?
Do you know   Bye   Nice to meet you   my name's
Have a good journey

A Hello, ¹_____ Geraldine.
B Hi. ²_____. I'm Vincenz.
A ³_____ Alessandro, my colleague?
B No. How do you do?
C ⁴_____ Nice to meet you.
…
C Our flight leaves soon. ⁵_____, Vincenz.
B Yes, nice meeting you, too.
⁶_____.
A Bye, and ⁷_____.
B ⁸_____.

Language at work

GRAMMAR REFERENCE

To be
Form
Positive:
> I **am/'m** a receptionist.
> You/We/They **are/'re** Polish.
> He/She/It **is/'s** from Brazil.

Negative:
> I **am not/'m not** a team leader.
> You/We/They **are not/aren't** Italian.
> He/She/It **is not/isn't** from South Africa.

Questions:
> **Am** I a personal assistant?
> **Are** you/we/they Brazilian?
> **Is** he/she/it from Italy?

Short answers:
> Yes, I **am**.
> Yes, you/we/they **are**.
> Yes, he/she/it **is**.
> No, I'**m not**.
> No, you/we/they **aren't**.
> No, he/she/it **isn't**.
> A **Are you** a financial director?
> B **No, I'm not.** I'm a receptionist.
> A **Is he** a technician?
> B **Yes, he is.**
> A **Are they** team leaders?
> B **No, they aren't. They're** personal assistants.
> A **Is it** an American product?
> B Yes, **it is**.

Possessives
Form
> I → my
> you → your
> he → his
> she → her
> it → its
> we → our
> they → their

Use
To say who has or owns something.
> I have a personal assistant. Greta is **my** personal assistant.
> Jonas has a company car. **His** car is a BMW.
> We have a good team. **Our** team is very small.

1 Complete the sentences, questions and answers.
1 _____ he Italian?
  No, he _____. He's Japanese.
2 _____ they Italian?
  No, they _____. They _____ Polish.
3 _____ Mirelle Brazilian?
  Yes, she _____.
4 The company _____ South African, it's British.
5 We _____ in Warsaw, in Poland.
6 _____ they technicians?
  Yes, they _____.
7 _____ you a personal assistant?
  Yes, I _____.
8 _____ Awad the CEO?
  No, he _____. He _____ the Financial Director.

2 Underline the correct words in *italics* to complete the sentences.
1 This is my department – Customer Service. Lawrie is *my / his* boss.
2 She has an assistant and *her / my* name is Pauline.
3 *Your / You* desk is next to Pauline's.
4 Next to you is Harald and those are *her / his* biscuits on his desk from a client.
5 The coffee machine is for *our / their* office only – not the whole department.
6 They have *their / my* coffee machine in the HR kitchen.

3 Complete the email with the words from the list.
am   your   my   our   are (x2)   *is* (x3)   *her*

Subject: my new company

Hi Abdul,

Here's the information about us:

The name of the company is IT-express.
It ¹_____ a computer company. I
²_____ the CEO, and my four colleagues
³_____ the technicians. Pascale is
⁴_____ personal assistant.

⁵_____ office is in Tunis, but the
customers ⁶_____ in Spain.

Yolanda ⁷_____ the new Sales Rep. She
⁸_____ Spanish, but ⁹_____ French
and English are very good.

Send me ¹⁰_____ phone number so we can meet.

Regards,

Kashyar

2 | Practice file

Working with words

1 Match 1–4 to a–d, then 5–7 to e–g to make sentences.

1 We employ ___
2 We export to ___
3 We produce ___
4 Customers buy ___

a the Asian market.
b our financial services from banks.
c 6,000 people at our company, worldwide.
d electronic components for computers.

5 We provide ___
6 We sell ___
7 We develop ___

e new technology for telecommunications.
f training for our software.
g our products to supermarkets.

2 Complete this crossword.

1 A _____ company finds new employees. (11 letters)
2 This company sells houses and offices. (4, 6 letters)
3 Banks provide us with _____ services. (9 letters)
4 Hotels and restaurants are in the _____ industry. (11 letters)
5 Samsung is an _____ company. (11 letters)
6 Microsoft produces this. (8 letters)
7 Car production is part of the _____ industry. (10 letters)

Business communication

1 Choose the correct answer, a or b.

1 Hello. Shen's Cars …
  a … What do you want?
  b … How can I help you?
2 Thanks for your help.
  a You're welcome.
  b Please.
3 Charlie Tieng speaking.
  a Hello Charlie. I am Matt.
  b Hello Charlie. It's Matt.
4 See you soon.
  a Yes, thanks.
  b See you.
5 Is Jo Harkett there, please?
  a Yes, I'll put you in.
  b Yes, I'll put you through.

2 Put each part of the phone conversation in the correct order 1–4.

1 a ___ Good afternoon. This is Clive Patrull from BHH. Is Rosa Barrera there, please?
  b ___ Thank you.
  c ___ Good afternoon. YC Windows. How can I help you?
  d ___ Yes, I'll put you through.

2 a ___ Hi, Clive. How are you?
  b ___ Hello. Rosa Barrera speaking.
  c ___ Fine, thanks. I'm calling about our meeting.
  d ___ Hi, Rosa. It's Clive Patrull.

3 a ___ OK, thanks. See you there.
  b ___ That's right.
  c ___ See you. Bye.
  d ___ So, it's conference room 2?

3 Complete the conversation with the correct words.

A Hello, Fast Training Solutions. [1]_____ can I [2]_____ you?
B Hello. [3]_____ is Madeline Roux from Mercier Insurance. I'm [4]_____ [5]_____ your IT training …
A … and I'll email you the price list.
B That's great. Thanks [6]_____ your [7]_____.
A [8]_____ welcome.
B Goodbye.
A Goodbye.

Language at work

GRAMMAR REFERENCE

Present simple

Form
Positive:
Subject + verb
> They **work** for Vodafone.
> She **works** for Vodafone.

Negative:
Subject + *do/does not* + verb
> I **don't/do not** *work for IBM.*
> He **doesn't/does not** *work for IBM.*

Questions:
Do/Does + subject + verb?
> **Do** *I/you/we/they* work for Unilever?
> **Does** *he/she/it* work for Unilever?

Short answers:
Yes/No + subject + *do/does/don't/doesn't.*
> Yes, I **do**.
> Yes, he **does**.
> No, they **don't**.
> No, it **doesn't**.

Careful: *I/he/she/it*: No -s on main verb in negative and question forms.

Spelling
Most verbs: *He/she/it* + verb + -*s*
> He work**s**, import**s**, sell**s**, buy**s**

Verbs ending in -*o*, -*ch*, -*ss*, -*sh*, -*x*: *He/she/it* + verb + -*es*
> She go**es**, watch**es**, miss**es**, wash**es**, fix**es**

Verbs with consonant + -*y*: replace the -*y* with -*ies*
> appl**y** → he appl**ies**, tr**y** → she tr**ies**, fl**y** → it fl**ies**

Exceptions: *Have* → *has*
Use
To talk about general facts.
> Glaxo **produces** pharmaceutical products.
> BMW **doesn't provide** financial services.
> **Do you produce** electronics? **No, I don't. I work** in the service industry.

---

1 Complete the questions with the correct form of the verbs in brackets. Then add a short answer.

1 A _____ you _____ (export) your products to France?
   B Yes, we _____.

2 A _____ they _____ (work) for GM?
   B Yes, they _____.

3 A _____ Remax _____ (sell) real estate?
   B Yes, it _____.

4 A _____ she _____ (provide) training for us?
   B No, she _____.

5 A _____ we _____ (employ) more than 10 nationalities in our company?
   B Yes, we _____.

6 A _____ you _____ (buy) products from your country?
   B No, I _____.

2 Complete the email with the correct form of the verbs from the list.

employ   have   produce   (not) work   sell   (not) export

To: Klaudia@bme.cz
From: s.field@bme.com
Subject: New customer information

Hello Klaudia,

Here's some information about your new customer: The company [1]_____ computer components. It [2]_____ 800 people in Europe. Its head office is in Toulouse. It [3]_____ to America, but it [4]_____ to most of Asia. We [5]_____ with their offices in the UK, but we [6]_____ contact with their factories in France and Italy.

Good luck with your meeting on Tuesday.

Sandy

3 Correct the mistakes in 1–7.

1 You do work for Terranova?
   _____

2 We imports most of our products.
   _____

3 Nokia doesn't works in the automobile industry.
   _____

4 Does Jane work for HSBC? Yes, she do.
   _____

5 Do you work in the recruitment industry? Yes, I work.
   _____

6 Max doesn't develops software. He provides software training.
   _____

7 Your company employs 500 people?
   _____

Working with words

1 Match the countries in the list to regions 1–6.

*Iran   France   Colombia   Morocco   Peru
Australia   Qatar   Singapore   The United States
Canada   Hungary   Botswana*

1 Latin America _____, _____
2 Europe _____, _____
3 North America _____, _____
4 Africa _____, _____
5 The Middle East _____, _____
6 Asia-Pacific _____, _____

2 Complete the text with words from the list.

*distribution centres   factories   sales offices
R&D centre   head office*

I work for an international company. Our
¹_____ is in Sweden –
that's where the management team works. Our
reps work from 30 ²_____
around the world, but we only have six
³_____ for our stock.
We make the products in the Far East – our
⁴_____ are in China, but our
main ⁵_____ is in India – this is
where we develop new products.

3 Match the words from **2** to definitions 1–5.

1 We make our products here.
_____

2 This is where we test the products and do research
and development. _____

3 When our sales reps aren't with a customer, they
work here. _____

4 The Management Department of the company
works here. _____

5 We deliver the products to customers from this
location. _____

Business communication

1 Put the conversation in the correct order 1–8.

a ___ Can I order some safety helmets, please?
b ___ Of course. It's Castell & Co.
c ___ Sorry, is that 40?
d ___ Good afternoon. Bentons Safety. How can I
help you?
e ___ Yes, of course. Can I have your company
name, please?
f ___ That's right. Can you deliver this week?
g ___ Sure. It's Y5-RS. And we'd like 40.
h ___ Castell & Co. And can you tell me the product
code, please?

2 Put the words in *italics* in the correct order to
continue the conversation from **1**.

A *but / in stock / I'm / don't / sorry / we / the Y5-RS / have*
¹_____. We can deliver on
Monday. Is that OK?

B OK, thanks. And *price / I / the / check / can*
²_____? Is it $5.35 for one?

A That's right. *address / delivery / your / What's*
³_____, please?

B It's 97 Light Avenue, Baltimore MD 21202.

A Sorry. *again / you / that / Can / say*
⁴_____, please?

B 97 Light Avenue, Baltimore MD 21202.

A Thanks. We'll deliver to that address on Monday.

B Great. *email / Can / my / order / confirm / by / you*
⁵_____, please?

A Of course. *email address / give / Can / me / you / your*
⁶_____, please?

B Yes. It's Phillipa underscore Wainwright at castellco
dot com.

A *that / say / you / slowly / more / Can*
⁷_____, please?

B Sure. It's Phillipa underscore Wainwright at
castellco dot com.

A Thanks. I'll send an email to confirm your order.

B Thanks very much.

A *for / Thanks / order / your*
⁸_____.

3 Choose the correct answer, a or b.

1 MMW. Can I help you?
a Hello. Can I order two laptops, please?
b Can you tell me your name, please?

2 Can you give me the prices, please?
a Can you spell that?   b Yes, of course.

3 Can you confirm by email, please?
a Sure, can you give me your email address?
b Can you speak more slowly?

4 My name's Wiktoria Poslavski.
a Sure, that's right.
b Can you spell that, please?

5 My phone number's 08392739.
a I'm sorry, but we don't have that in stock.
b Can you speak more slowly, please?

Language at work

GRAMMAR REFERENCE

There is / There are

there is / there isn't + singular noun
> **There's a** factory in Beijing.
> **There isn't an** office in Africa.

there are / there aren't + plural noun
> **There are factories** all over the world.
> **There aren't any offices** in Asia and Europe.

Questions:
Invert *is/are* and *there*.
> **Is there** a factory in America?
> **Are there** offices in Croatia?

Short answers:
Don't repeat the subject.
> A *Is there an office in Bahrain?*
> B *Yes,* **there is.**
> A *Are there a lot of employees?*
> B *No,* **there aren't.**

Some/any

Use *some/any* with plural nouns.
Use *some* in positive sentences.
> There are **some products** in the distribution centre.

Use *any* in negative sentences and questions.
> There **aren't any products** in the sales office.
> **Are there any managers** in the technical centre?

---

1 Read the information and complete the questions and answers 1–7.

In Cairo Conference and Exhibition Centre	Near to Cairo Conference and Exhibition Centre
1,200 parking spaces	Shops
Chinese garden	Banks
3 large meeting rooms	5-star hotels
Restaurants	Airport

1 Are there any restaurants in the Conference Centre? Yes, _____.
2 Are there any shops in the Conference Centre? _____.
3 _____ hotels near the Conference Centre? _____.
4 Is there a bank in the Conference Centre? _____.
5 _____ meeting rooms? _____.
6 _____ parking spaces? _____.
7 Is there an airport near the Conference Centre? _____.

2 Complete the email with *some/any* or *a/an*.

Dear Brioni,

Our visitors arrive on Thursday. Please check we have everything ready.

FOOD:
There are ^{1}_____ drinks in the meeting room – are there ^{2}_____ biscuits? There aren't ^{3}_____ sandwiches for lunch, but there is ^{4}_____ restaurant near the office.

MEETING ROOMS:
There's ^{5}_____ video projector and ^{6}_____ pens and paper. There isn't ^{7}_____ laptop and there isn't ^{8}_____ wireless connection.

ARRIVING:
Are there ^{9}_____ parking spaces in the car park for them? There are ^{10}_____ name cards for them and ^{11}_____ info pack about the company at Reception.

Thanks,

J

3 Tick (✓) the correct sentence, a or b.
1 a There are three factories in Europe and one in Asia.
   b There's three factories in Europe and one in Asia.
2 a There aren't any sales reps in China.
   b There are any sales reps in China.
3 a There are some managers in the technical centre and some in head office.
   b There is some managers in the technical centre and some in head office.
4 a There isn't some distribution centre in the UK.
   b There isn't a distribution centre in the UK.
5 a There isn't any sales office in Dubai.
   b There isn't a sales office in Dubai.
6 a Are there a computer programmer here?
   b Are there any computer programmers here?
7 a Is there a receptionist in the technical centre? Yes, there are.
   b Is there a receptionist in the technical centre? Yes, there is.
8 a Is there a car park at the distribution centre? Yes, there isn't.
   b Is there a car park at the distribution centre? No, there isn't.

Working with words

1 Complete the sentences with words from the list.

battery   contact   select   username
password   button   mobile

1 Key in the phone number and press the green
_____ .

2 First, _____ an account to send the money
from.

3 Your _____ for the website is the same as your
email address.

4 A Can I recharge my phone _____ here?
B Sure, there's a power point over there.

5 You aren't in my _____ list. Can you tell me
your phone number, please?

6 You can use someone's phone number to send
money with _____ banking.

7 Do you know the Wi-fi _____ to get Internet
access in the hotel room?

2 Match 1–6 to a–f to make sentences.

1 To begin, click ___
2 It's easy to access ___
3 I can't log ___
4 How do I link ___
5 To start, download ___
6 You need to register ___

a in to my emails.
b my phone to my laptop?
c your device to use mobile banking.
d the app to your smartphone or tablet.
e your bank account on your mobile phone.
f on 'start'.

3 ~~Cross out~~ one noun in *italics* which you cannot use
with the verb in **bold**.

1 I need to **charge** my *battery / laptop / screen /*
smartphone / tablet / device.

2 I can't **access** *the Internet / my username /*
my emails / my bank account / our website.

3 I want to **send** *Wi-fi / money / a text message /*
payment / an SMS.

4 **Press** *the button / your account / 'confirm'.*

5 Please **key in** *your username / your order number /*
your device / your password.

Business communication

1 Complete the missing words in the four
conversations.

A Can you ¹g_____ m_____ a h_____?
B Sure.
A I ²d_____ k_____ h_____ t_____
put these photos onto CD-ROM. I'm ³t_____
t_____ copy them for Bob. Can you
⁴h_____ m_____?

C Yes, ⁵o_____ c_____.
D ⁶H_____ d_____ I send a file to Sandy?

C Let me see.
E Do you ⁷w_____ a h_____?
F That ⁸w_____ b_____ g_____. I don't
know how to log on.

G I'm trying to download a document.
H Can I ⁹h_____?
G Oh, ¹⁰y_____, p_____.
H Click on that icon and …

2 Put the conversations in the correct order.

A
a ___ Sure.
b ___ I've got a problem. I'm trying to book a flight
on the Internet, but it doesn't work.
c ___ John, can you help me?
d ___ Yes, but I don't know how to enter it.
e ___ Do you have a username for the website?
f ___ Click here, then key it in.

B
a ___ That would be good.
b ___ What's the problem?
c ___ How do I print this document?
d ___ Let me see …
e ___ Are you OK, Galina? Do you want a hand?

3 Underline the correct responses in *italics*.

1 A Do you want a hand?
B *That would be good. / Yes, of course.*

2 A Can you give me a hand?
B *Yes, please. / Sure.*

3 A Can you help me?
B *Yes, of course. / That would be good.*

4 A Can I help?
B *Yes, of course. / Yes, please.*

Language at work

> **GRAMMAR REFERENCE**
>
> ## Adverbs of frequency
>
> ### Form
>
> The adverb of frequency goes **before** the main verb.
>
> *I **never work** 10 hours a day.*
>
> *He **always takes** a break.*
>
> The adverb of frequency goes **after** the verb *be*.
>
> *I **am never** late.*
>
> *He **is always** late.*
>
> *You **are sometimes** sick.*
>
> ### Use
>
> To describe how regularly someone does something.
>
> *never   rarely   sometimes   often   usually   always*
>
> 0% •————————— 50% —————————• 100%
>
> ## Questions (present simple)
>
> ### Form
>
> Question word + *do/does* + subject + verb phrase.
>
> *Who **do** you work for?*
>
> *What **does** she do?*
>
> *Where **do** they live?*
>
> See also **Practice file 2** for other question forms in the present simple.
>
> ### Meaning
>
> To ask about:
>
> The way/method
>
> *How do you travel to work? By train.*
>
> People/a company you work for
>
> *Who does she work for? Philips.*
>
> General information
>
> *What do they do? They sell electronics.*
>
> Frequency
>
> *How often does he take a holiday? Once a year.*
>
> A place
>
> *Where do you work? In Singapore.*
>
> The reason
>
> *Why do they like the company? The pay is very good.*
>
> A time
>
> *When do we start work? At 8.00 a.m.*

1 The chart shows the number of days the employees were late for work last month. Complete the sentences about the employees with the words from the list.

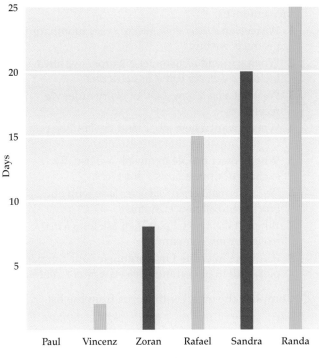

sometimes   never   rarely   always   usually   often

1 Paul is _____ late for work.

2 Sandra is _____ late for work.

3 Zoran is _____ late for work.

4 Vincenz is _____ late for work.

5 Randa is _____ late for work.

6 Rafael is _____ late for work.

2 Put the words in *italics* in the correct order.

1 *She / break / takes / always / a*

_____ at 10 00.

2 *We're / sick / rarely* _____.

3 *They / never / seven / days / work*

_____ a week.

4 *I / off / take / usually / Friday*

_____.

5 *We / finish / work / sometimes*

_____ at 16.00.

6 *He's / late / for / work / often*

_____.

3 Match questions 1–6 to answers a–f.

1 When do you have lunch? ___

2 How often do you go to work by train? ___

3 What does your company do? ___

4 Who do you work with? ___

5 Where do you take a break? ___

6 Why do you like your job? ___

a I usually go to the canteen for a coffee.

b At 12.00.

c It's very interesting.

d Never, I always drive.

e I have three colleagues in my team.

f It develops software.

Working with words

1 <u>Underline</u> the correct words in *italics* to complete the sentences.

1 We receive *a letter / an invoice* every month for the products we buy.

2 When we send a customer his order, we always include a *delivery note / business card*.

3 We print a *hard copy / CV* of every order we receive.

4 When I want a new job, I send my *business card / CV* to companies that interest me.

5 When I meet people in my job, we usually exchange *business cards / order forms*.

6 We send *a hard copy / an order form* with our brochure to all new customers.

7 When I take a taxi, I pay, then ask for a *letter / receipt* for my company.

8 If you are interested in working for our company, please fill in our online *application form / contract*.

2 Complete the email with words from the list.

save   print   receive   open   send   forward

To: José_Pablo@blc.com
From: Tiler.macintyre@blc.com
Subject: Organizing paperwork /
PC problems!

Hello José,

There are a few IT problems in our office today, so can you do me a favour?

Can you ¹_____ a hard copy of the report from the meeting and give it to Amanda? I also need a copy – can you ²_____ the document to me in your next email?

Also, I can't ³_____ our customer correspondence folder. If you can, please ⁴_____ the order forms in this folder.
Can you ⁵_____ me the invoice from Bertrands so I have their contact details, please?

Finally, can you call me when you ⁶_____ this email?

I don't know if my email is working!

Thanks,

T

---

3 ~~Cross out~~ the verb in 1–4 that doesn't match the noun in **bold**.

1 receive / attach / print   **an email**
2 receive / print / open   **a business card**
3 forward / print / receive   **a hard copy**
4 open / save / print   **a folder**

Business communication

1 Complete the conversations with expressions from the lists.

A

*You need to   I'll speak to   There are some problems with
That would be great   explain the situation*

A ¹_____ the equipment and the products aren't ready for the Polish order. Can you help?

B ²_____ contact the customer and ³_____.

A OK.

B ⁴_____ the service engineers.

A ⁵_____.

B

*We did, but   I'll call   You need to   for your help
No problem   We can't   I'll explain*

A ⁶_____ find the invoice for Delaney & Co. They want a special price.

B ⁷_____ call Jenny in the Accounts Department.

A ⁸_____ she wasn't in the office.

B ⁹_____ the customer then. Do they normally have a special price?

A No, not usually.

B OK. ¹⁰_____ the situation.

A That's great. Thanks a lot ¹¹_____.

B ¹²_____.

2 Complete the expressions and find the hidden message.

1 We n _ _ | _ | to fix the problem.
2 Don't w | _ | _ _ _.
3 I'll e _ _ _ _ _ | _ | the situation.
4 That would be g _ _ _ | _ |

5 We've got a | _ | _ _ _ _ _ _ with the order.
6 I'll c | _ | _ _ the customer now.
7 We c _ | _ | _ deliver in time.
8 We changed the software, but it d | _ | _ _ _ work.
9 I'll let you know as soon as I | _ | _ _.

Language at work

GRAMMAR REFERENCE

Past simple: *be*

Form

Positive: Subject + *was/were* ...

> I/He/She/It **was** at the presentation.
> You/We/They **were** at the presentation.

Negative: Subject + *was not / were not* ...

> I/He/She/It **wasn't** in the office.
> You/We/They **weren't** in the office.

Questions: (Question word*) + *was/were/wasn't/weren't* + subject ...?

> **Was she** in the office?
> **Why weren't you** at work?

Past simple: regular verbs

Form

Positive: Subject + verb + *-ed* ...

> I **worked** for Vodafone.
> They **talked** about branding.

Negative: Subject + *did not / didn't* + verb ...

> They **didn't like** the presentation.
> You **did not ask** any questions.

Questions: (Question word*) + *did/didn't* + subject + verb ...?

> **Did** she **work** for Unilever?
> **When did** you **leave** your last job?

Short answers: Don't repeat the main verb.

> A *Did she work for Unilever?*
> B *Yes, she **did**.*

*See **Practice file 4** for question words.

Spelling

Most regular verbs: verb + *-ed*

> start → started

Verbs ending in *-e*: verb + *-d*

> decide → decided

Verbs ending in consonant-vowel-consonant: double the last letter + *-ed*

> stop → stopped

Verbs ending in consonant + *-y*: replace *-y* with *-ied*

> try → tried

Use

To talk about a finished action in the past. We usually know when the action/event happened or didn't happen.

> I **was** at the meeting last week.
> I **received** your message yesterday.
> You **didn't send** me the document.

To ask when an action in the past took place.

> When **did** the conference **start**?

1 Underline the correct words in *italics* to complete the conversation.

A How ¹*was / were* the meeting?

B I don't know, I ²*wasn't / weren't* there. I ³*was / were* on holiday, but John emailed me the notes from the meeting. It ⁴*was / were* very long!

A I'm glad I ⁵*were / was* off sick then! Remi and Anna ⁶*were / was* also away. They ⁷*were / was* on a skiing holiday, but there ⁸*wasn't / weren't* any snow!

2 Put the words in 1–5 in the correct order to make questions, then match them to answers a–e.

1 they / weren't / why / the / at / meeting

_____?

2 interesting / was / it

_____?

3 questions / were / many / there

_____?

4 was / last / your / when / business trip

_____?

5 at / who / the / meeting / was

_____?

a Yes, it was.
b Last Friday.
c They were in Los Angeles.
d Max and Yolanda.
e No, there weren't.

3 Complete the text with the past simple form of the verbs in brackets.

> ### Report: Seminar Hotel Booking
>
> We ¹_____ (decide) to use Travel Inn. I ²_____ (call) to ask for a special price and they ³_____ (email) me back to say it ⁴_____ (not be) possible. We ⁵_____ (not contact) them again and ⁶_____ (try) another hotel. Two days later, we ⁷_____ (receive) an email from Travel Inn. They ⁸_____ (be) sorry about the prices and ⁹_____ (offer) us a 10% discount. I ¹⁰_____ (book) the meeting room immediately and they ¹¹_____ (confirm) this in writing. It ¹²_____ (be) exactly what we ¹³_____ (want).

4 Make questions in the past simple using the prompts.

1 When / you / start work?

_____

2 Where / she / go on holiday?

_____

3 Why / you / not email / me?

_____

4 How / you / contact her?

_____

5 Who / they / speak to?

_____

6 Why / we / not call / him?

_____

Working with words

1 Match 1–6 to a–f to make questions and sentences.

1 Are you ___
2 I like to comment ___
3 You can build ___
4 I want to connect ___
5 You can search ___
6 Why don't you join ___

a for the HR Manager's profile.
b a network of useful contacts.
c on LinkedIn?
d a professional group?
e on interesting posts.
f with old friends from school.

2 Complete the conversation with the words from the list.

posts   bio   on   follows   networking
add   tweets   search

A Are you ¹_____ Twitter?
B No, I don't have time for social ²_____.
A But it's easy to join and fast to use. You just write your ³_____, so everyone knows who you are. Then you can send ⁴_____.
B What are they?
A Short messages – like ⁵_____ on other social networks – but you can only use a maximum of 140 characters. That's why it's fast!
B And who reads my tweets?
A Anyone who ⁶_____ you. You can ⁷_____ for people and ⁸_____ them to the list of people you are following.
B Mmm. I'm not sure …

3 ~~Cross out~~ one noun in *italics* which you cannot use with the social media verb in **bold**.

1 You can **join** a *conversation / profile / group / social network*.
2 You can **update** your *status / chat / bio / profile*.
3 You can **add** a *status / link / friend / comment*.
4 You can **like** a *post / page / search / photo*.
5 You can **share** a *photo / post / link / friend*.

Business communication

1 <u>Underline</u> the correct expressions in *italics* to complete the conversation.

A Hello, I'm Rachel. ¹*Can I join you? / Can I help you?*
B ²*Yes, of course. / No, I don't.*
A ³*I hear you work for / Is this your first time* at the congress?
B No, I was here last year. ⁴*What do you think of it? / Please take a seat.*
A It's really interesting and nice to meet new people.

2 ~~Cross out~~ the extra word in each expression in *italics*.

A Hi, I'm Mia Pieczek from Slovakia. ¹*I hear you do work for Motorola.*
B ²*Yes, that's is right.*
A You're my customer in Slovakia! ³*Would you like get another coffee?*
B ⁴*No, you're thanks.* I'm fine.
A OK. Well, I'd like one, so I'll ⁵*see me you later.*
B Yes. ⁶*Nice to talking to you.*

3 Put the words in the correct order to make questions and sentences.

1 join / can / you / I

_____?

2 you / hear / I / for / KPMG / work

_____.

3 something / get / can / you / I

_____?

4 you / think / exhibition / what / of / the / do

_____?

5 me / please / excuse

_____.

Language at work

1 Match verbs 1–10 to their past simple forms a–j.

1 do ___	a went
2 take ___	b took
3 give ___	c met
4 spend ___	d left
5 meet ___	e gave
6 go ___	f had
7 fly ___	g spent
8 have ___	h did
9 leave ___	i saw
10 see ___	j flew

2 Complete the email using the past simple form of the verbs in brackets.

Subject: Trip to Hawaii – I'm back!

Hi Timo,

I'm back from the trip. It was great. We 1_____ (fly) with United Airlines in Business Class! Julio 2_____ (meet) us at the airport when we arrived. We 3_____ (spend) two weeks visiting customers, which was very interesting. Then we 4_____ (have) a short holiday and 5_____ (do) some sightseeing. We 6_____ (not see) Heike unfortunately – we 7_____ (leave) before she 8_____ (come) back from her holiday.

Anyway, can you tell me what happened in the company in the last three weeks?

Thanks,

Clio

3 Look at the diary. Complete the sentences using the past simple and the time expressions from the list. Today is Wednesday 11th.

last Thursday   yesterday   last night
a week ago   two days ago

MON 2	TUES 3	WEDS 4	THURS 5	FRI 6
		Go to Warsaw	Give presentation to the Board	

MON 9	TUES 10	WEDS 11	THURS 12	FRI 13
Leave Warsaw	Meet Jakob for lunch 8 p.m. see the new Bond film			

1 I _____ to Warsaw
_____.

2 I _____ a presentation to the Board _____.

3 I _____ Warsaw
_____.

4 I _____ Jakob for lunch
_____.

5 I _____ the new Bond film
_____.

Working with words

1 Complete the text with the correct option (a, b or c).
This is my department. We ¹___ customer orders. Ahmed ²___ the team and he ³___ our work. Our department helps to ⁴___ our products. We tell customers about new products when we receive orders. I ⁵___ the financial side: invoices and payment. I ⁶___ the invoices are correct and ⁷___ customers about problems with payment. The Logistics Department ⁸___ our work. They deliver the orders to the customers.

1	a develop	5	a deal with
	b deal with		b contact
	c promote		c develop
2	a is responsible for	6	a support
	b contacts		b am responsible for
	c checks		c check
3	a develops	7	a contact
	b promotes		b promote
	c organizes		c am responsible for
4	a develop	8	a checks
	b promote		b supports
	c organize		c develops

2 Complete the crossword with the names of departments.

1 is responsible for deliveries (9 letters)
2 makes the products (10 letters)
3 deals with questions and problems from customers: Customer _____ (8 letters)
4 promotes the company's products (9 letters)
5 develops new products: _____ and Development (8 letters)
6 is responsible for the money in the company (7 letters)
7 deals with the employees: _____ Resources (5 letters)
8 is responsible for the computer network: Information _____ (10 letters)

Business communication

1 Who says these expressions? Write caller (*C*) or receiver (*R*).
1 Can she call me back? ___
2 Can I take a message? ___
3 My number is 759 3810. ___
4 Can I have a contact number? ___
5 Could I leave a message? ___
6 I'd like to speak to Lena-Maria, please. ___
7 I'm sorry, but he isn't here today. ___
8 I'll give him your message. ___

2 Complete the conversation with the questions from the list.

Can I take a message?   Can I have a contact number?
Can she call me back?   So that's 0747 58360?
Is Galina there, please?

A Jocelyn speaking. Can I help you?
B Hi. ¹_____
A I'm sorry, but she isn't available.
   ²_____
B Yes, please. I'm calling about our order.
   ³_____
A Sure. ⁴_____
B Yes, it's 07747 58360. The name's Tiernan.
A ⁵_____
B No, it's 077 – double 7.

3 Put the words in *italics* in the correct order to complete the conversation.
A ADAC. Good morning.
B Hello. *Could / I / to / speak*
   ¹_____ Adira Chen, please?
A *I'm / she's / but / sorry* ²_____
   in a meeting.
B Oh. *Could / leave / a / I / message*
   ³_____?
A Sure.
B My name's Vrajkishore Kundu and my number is 08274 38573. *Can / back / call / me / she*
   ⁴_____ as soon as possible?
A So that's Mr Kundu, phone number 08274 38573. *Is / right / that* ⁵_____?
B That's right.
A *I'll / message / her / give / your*
   ⁶_____.

Language at work

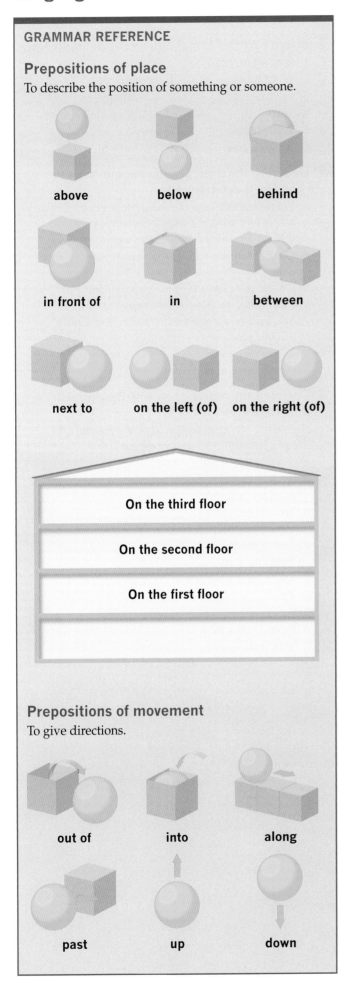

GRAMMAR REFERENCE

Prepositions of place
To describe the position of something or someone.

above   below   behind

in front of   in   between

next to   on the left (of)   on the right (of)

On the third floor

On the second floor

On the first floor

Prepositions of movement
To give directions.

out of   into   along

past   up   down

1 You are on the stairs. Look at the plan and complete the sentences with the words from the list.

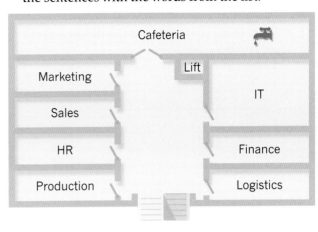

on the right   on the left   behind   on
in   next to   between   in front of

1 Production is _____ HR.
2 Finance is _____ Logistics and IT.
3 You are _____ the first floor.
4 The water fountain is _____ the cafeteria.
5 Logistics is _____.
6 Marketing is the last door _____.
7 The lift is _____ the cafeteria.
8 Marketing is _____ Sales.

2 Read these directions and look at the plan and information in 1. Where do the directions take you?
1 Start at the stairs. Go past HR and then turn left. _____
2 Go left out of IT and along the corridor. They are in front of you. _____
3 Go out of the cafeteria, turn right and go into the room. _____
4 Go into the lift and up one floor. _____

3 Correct the mistakes in *italics*.
Business Tower. JEB Electronics. Our offices:
We are *in* [1]_____ the 15th floor. Lifts are *in front* [2]_____ Reception. Take the lift to the 15th floor and turn left – *in* [3]_____ the right is a coffee area. *Next* [4]_____ the coffee area is a meeting room. Go *along* [5]_____ the meeting room on your right. We are *between of* [6]_____ the meeting room and the stairs. Finance and HR are *below* [7]_____ on the 16th floor.
Car parking is underground – *above* [8]_____ the offices. Ask for a pass at the security desk *on right* [9]_____ before you drive in.

Working with words

1 Complete the sentences and use the answers to complete the crossword.

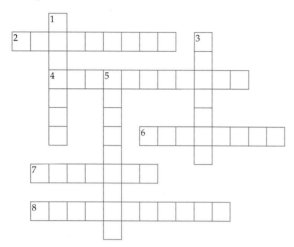

1 As a doctor, I must be _____ about the medicines I give to my patients. (7 letters)

2 My project manager often has problems to deal with, but she is very _____, and usually solves them. (9 letters)

3 I spend a lot of time looking at numbers and budgets. It's not always easy to stay _____. (7 letters)

4 When I started in my company six years ago, I wasn't very _____, but now I know all about the job. (11 letters)

5 In my job, you have to think quickly and be really _____. (9 letters)

6 It is important to stay _____ with the customers. (8 letters)

7 People don't always understand about IT, so I have to be _____ when I try to explain how things work. (7 letters)

8 When we interview for new advertising executives, we look for people who are _____. (11 letters)

2 Complete the conversation with the phrases from the list.

isn't very good   has a lot of experience in   good at
doesn't have any experience in   a qualification in

A We're looking for an advertising assistant and we have a strong candidate. She has
¹_____ marketing.
She is imaginative and energetic, but she
²_____ our product range.

B I don't think that's a problem – she can learn that. She's ³_____ organizing and planning. I saw some of her work at the interview. She also ⁴_____ managing people.

A Yes, but she ⁵_____ at presenting – she was terrible at the interview.

B She can do a presentation course to help her though.

Business communication

1 Match 1–6 to a–f to make questions and sentences.

1 Can we arrange ___   a Monday.
2 What time ___   b good for you?
3 I'm free on ___   c a meeting?
4 Sorry, ___   d at lunchtime?
5 Is 10.00 a.m. ___   e are you free?
6 Are you free ___   f I'm busy then.

2 Underline the correct expressions in *italics* to complete the conversation.

A We need to discuss the sales conference. ¹*Can we arrange a meeting? / I can't meet on Tuesday.*

B OK, ²*is Thursday OK? / I can't meet then.*

A Oh, no, ³*are you busy at 5.00 p.m.? / sorry, I'm busy then.*

B OK, well Wednesday's no good for me, but ⁴*I can't meet then. / are you free on Friday?*

A Yes. Friday's fine for me. ⁵*Is 11.00 a.m. OK? / 12.00 is good.*

B 11 a.m. is good.

A Great. See you on Friday, then.

3 Complete the conversation with the expressions from the list.

can't meet   Wednesday's good   Wednesday OK
Are you busy on   What time are you free
We need to meet about   is fine

A ¹_____ the problem with the product design.

B Yes, of course. ²_____ Tuesday?

A Yes, in the morning. I ³_____ until 2.00 p.m.

B 2.00 p.m. is a bit late. Is ⁴_____?

A Yes, ⁵_____.

B ⁶_____?

A From 11.00 a.m.

B 11.00 a.m. ⁷_____ for me.

Language at work

GRAMMAR REFERENCE

Present continuous

Form

Positive: Subject + *am/is/are* + *-ing*
> I **am/'m writing** the monthly report.
> He **is/'s working** from home.
> They **are/'re meeting** the MD.

Negative: Subject + *am / is / are not* + *-ing*
> I **am not / 'm not working** at home today.
> She **is not / isn't having** her lunch.
> You **are not / aren't talking** to Security.

Questions: (Question word) + *am/is/are* + subject + *-ing*?
> **Am I working** with the new customer today?
> **Is it raining** today?
> **Are we looking** at the right report?

Short answers: Don't repeat the main verb.
> A *Am I working with the new customer today?*
> B *Yes, you are.*
> A *Are we looking at the right report?*
> B *No, we aren't.*

Spelling

Most verbs: add *-ing* to the verb
> *study → studying / start → starting*

Verbs ending with *-e*: replace *-e* with *-ing*
> *arrive → arriving*

Verbs ending with vowel + consonant: double the last consonant and add *-ing*
> *stop → stopping*

Use

To describe an action or event in progress around the time of speaking.
> *Are you **working** on any interesting new projects?*

To describe an action happening at the moment of speaking.
> A *What **are** you **doing**?*
> B *We're **checking** all the new application forms.*

---

1 Complete the email using the present continuous form of the verbs in brackets.

> **Subject:** New position questions/update
>
> Hi Max,
>
> Here's some information about the new position:
>
> Talvinder can't take the new job because she [1]_____ (finish) her university studies. We [2]_____ (contact) some of the other applicants from the interviews last week.
>
> Janis [3]_____ (check) their qualifications again and I [4]_____ (arrange) second interviews. We [5]_____ (not invite) applicants from abroad – this takes too long.
>
> I need some help from you with the interviews – do you have time or [6]_____ (you plan) the HR conference at the moment? Please let me know.
>
> Regards,
>
> F

2 Put the conversation in the correct order 1–7.

a ___ I know, but Konrad is waiting for this. Anyway, what's Abi's news?

b ___ Are you coming to the meeting now?

c ___ He's helping set up a new sales office in Cape Town.

d ___ No, sorry. I'm working on this presentation.

e ___ Well, he isn't managing the sales team any more.

f ___ But Abi is here from South Africa – he's only staying three days.

g ___ What's he doing now, then?

3 Correct the mistakes in 1–6.

1 Where Zoran and Judith going?
_____

2 They're do a course on presentations at the InterContinental today.
_____

3 Are you go to the party?
_____

4 Does he working in Paris this month?
_____

5 We training to become software engineers.
_____

6 Are they stay at the Dorchester Hotel?
_____

Working with words

1 Complete the email with the words from the list.

up-to-date   *fast*   *wide*   *low*   *friendly*   *high*

> ✉
>
> Our ¹_____ range of products is of
> ²_____ quality and we always offer
> ³_____ prices. We produce our products
> using modern machines and ⁴_____
> technology. You can see all the products in
> our brochure and read about our ⁵_____
> delivery times and ⁶_____ customer
> service.
>
> Please call us or order online.

2 Choose the correct adjective (a, b or c) to complete 1–6.

1 We use ___ technology to build our systems.
  a friendly   b low   c up-to-date
2 Don't buy from BNS, their prices are too ___.
  a high   b fast   c bad
3 We have a ___ choice of products.
  a up-to-date   b wide   c high
4 Our new offices are in a ___ location.
  a slow   b good   c wide
5 We offer a ___ delivery time for urgent orders.
  a fast   b expensive c good
6 They are expensive, but they produce ___-quality products.
  a wide   b bad   c high

3 Put the letters in *italics* in the correct order to make words to complete the presentation.

We are very competitive and are number two
in the market. Why? We offer *findlrey* ¹_____
customer service. We can guarantee a fast
dylvreei tmie ²_____ for our products and,
although they are sometimes *epxnseiev* ³_____,
the products are high *qyultai* ⁴_____ and there is a
wide *coihce* ⁵_____. The customer service office is
also in a *odog* ⁶_____ location for our customers.

Business communication

1 <u>Underline</u> the correct words in *italics* to complete the conversation.

A I have two quotes here for office printers. It's difficult to choose one.
B How do they ¹*compare / better*?
A Lexi is ²*difference / similar* to Samsonic.
B So what's the ³*difference / compare*?
A The ⁴*advantage / better* of the Lexi is it works with a wireless network.
B That sounds good.
A Yes, but it's more expensive.
B The Samsonic is cheaper, but the ⁵*comparison / disadvantage* is it is more difficult to use and isn't wireless.
A I ⁶*choice / prefer* the Lexi – it's a higher price but better for our office.
B OK.

2 Put this conversation in the correct order 1–7. The first and last lines are correct.

a _1_ A I have two hotels that look good. Which should we book?
b ___ B Let's choose Mercure – breakfast is included, we have transport and we can get a taxi to the centre of town.
c ___ A Well, Mercure is similar to Ibis. Mercure has breakfast included, but Ibis doesn't.
d ___ B How do they compare?
e ___ A Exactly. But the disadvantage of Ibis is it only has a suite free – no single rooms.
f ___ B So we don't need a hire car?
g ___ A Yes, breakfast is good, but the advantage of Ibis is its location. It's more central.
h ___ B Well, I'd like breakfast in the price.
i ___ B Oh, does Mercure have single rooms?
j ___ A Yes, and the advantage of Mercure is we can have free pick up from the airport.
k _11_ A OK – I'll book it.

Language at work

GRAMMAR REFERENCE

Comparatives

Form

One-syllable adjectives (also some two-syllable adjectives)

Adjectives ending in a consonant: add -er

   fast → *faster*

Adjectives ending in -e: add -r

   wide → *wider*

Adjectives ending in a vowel + consonant: double the consonant and add -er

   big → *bigger*

Adjectives ending in -y: replace the -y with -ier

   easy → *easier*

Long adjectives – two syllables or more

Put *more* **before** the adjective. The adjective doesn't change.

   difficult → *more difficult*

Irregular adjectives

   good → *better*

   bad → *worse*

Use

Use comparatives to compare two or more things or people.

   *Shopping online gives you a **wider** choice of products and **cheaper** prices than shopping on the high street.*

Than

To compare two things use *than* after the adjective.

   *A Daewoo is **cheaper than** an Audi.*

   *Sofitel is **more expensive than** Novotel.*

   *Express delivery is **faster than** standard delivery.*

1 Put the adjectives from the list in the correct category 1–3. Then add their comparative forms.

*friendly   expensive   low   experienced
easy   difficult   fast   cheap*

Adjective	Comparative
1 _____ _____ _____	+ -er _____ _____ _____
2 _____ _____	+ -ier _____ _____
3 _____ _____ _____	+ more _____ _____ _____

2 Correct the mistakes in 1–8.

1 easyJet is often more cheap than British Airways. _____

2 Vodafone offers a gooder service than my phone provider. _____

3 Our office is in a more expensive location like our competitor's. _____

4 Spanish is easyer to learn than Japanese. _____

5 Our customers are often more experienced that our technicians. _____

6 The competitors offer more lower prices than us. _____

7 The new mobile phone is more difficulter to use than the old model. _____

8 Their customer service is worser than before. _____

3 Complete the text with the words from the list.

*friendlier   higher   expensive   wider   than
more (x2)   easier   better   worse*

Report: Our market position in comparison to our competitor in the supermarket business.

- Our products are often [1]_____ expensive, but we offer a [2]_____ choice [3]_____ them.
- Quality of our products is always [4]_____ than theirs.
- Their sales staff are well trained and [5]_____ experienced than our shop assistants.
- Customers say our staff are [6]_____ than the competitor's.
- Our stores are in more [7]_____ locations, but we are [8]_____ to find than the competitor.
- In conclusion, it's not possible to say we are [9]_____ or [10]_____ than our competitor. We have different qualities.

Working with words

1 Complete the email with the words from the list.

decisions   ideas   solutions
problems   in a team   meetings

Subject: My new job!

Hi Xander,

My new job's great – I'm so glad I moved departments. In this job we work ¹_____. I'm the assistant to the technicians who find ²_____ for our customers. I don't make ³_____ or solve ⁴_____, but it's my job to tell the team about changes and new systems. Sometimes I attend ⁵_____ where we work together to develop ⁶_____ for the future. It makes a nice change to be part of a team.

How's your job?

---

2 Complete the sentences, then find the words in the word search.

1 I usually _____ a meeting every Tuesday.
2 It was a _____ decision to close the factory.
3 I called the Helpdesk because I had a _____ problem.
4 Our bosses want us to _____ solutions to our customers' problems.
5 We have more ideas when we _____ in a team.
6 At the brainstorming meetings we _____ ideas for marketing campaigns.
7 Lenny had some _____ ideas for the team-building weekend.
8 Roberto must _____ the right decisions so the project doesn't cost more money.
9 We have ten urgent orders and there's a transport strike – we don't know how to _____ the problem.
10 The company doesn't allow Internet surfing – that's HR's _____ decision.

I	G	H	L	F	F	D	L	J	A
H	V	E	U	X	E	I	A	O	U
W	B	E	E	V	W	F	N	H	E
X	Q	K	E	Z	A	F	I	D	Q
U	A	L	Z	E	C	I	F	G	Y
M	O	X	F	E	S	C	D	O	U
P	W	O	R	K	V	U	R	O	H
D	N	E	T	T	A	L	T	D	B
B	V	J	J	U	W	T	O	I	L
N	I	P	T	S	W	U	G	S	Y

Business communication

1 Complete the conversation with the expressions from the list.

Do you think   I think   What do you think
my opinion   Yes, I agree

A ¹_____ about our new advertisement?
B ²_____ it's the best one so far.
A ³_____.
B ⁴_____ the picture is big enough?
A Oh yes, but in ⁵_____, the logo should be smaller.

2 Put the words in *italics* in the correct order to continue the conversation from **1**.

B I / agree / don't ¹_____. The logo is the most important thing. I like the colours of the packaging – *opinion / your / what's* ²_____?
A *not / I'm / sure / so* ³_____.
B *I / we / should / think* ⁴_____ make the packaging more interesting with the same colours.
A *true / That's* ⁵_____. It's not the most attractive box for such a great product.

3 Underline the correct words in *italics* to complete the conversations.

1 A What's your opinion?
  B *That's true. / Well, I think …*
2 A I think we should change suppliers.
  B *What do you think? / I'm not so sure.*
3 A I don't think that's a good idea.
  B *I disagree. / In my opinion.*
4 A What do you think?
  B *That's true. / In my opinion, …*
5 A In my opinion, it's a waste of time.
  B *I think we should. / Yes, I agree.*

4 Correct the mistakes in 1–5.

1 What you think? _____
2 That true. _____
3 Do think our company is the best?
  _____
4 I not so sure. _____
5 My opinion, we should stop production.
  _____

Language at work

1 Complete the conversation with the superlative form of the adjectives in brackets.

A We need to book the hotel. We've got a few to choose from. Which one do you think is [1]_____ (good)?

B Well, the Meridian is [2]_____ (easy) to get to, and it's [3]_____ (modern).

A Yes, but it's also [4]_____ (expensive).

B True, but this is a very important event. Price isn't [5]_____ (important) thing. The Meridian has [6]_____ (high) quality service, [7]_____ (big) meeting room and [8]_____ (wide) choice of food.

A OK, let's book it.

2 Put the adjectives from the list in the correct row 1–13 in the table and then add their superlative forms.

fast   *good*   *friendly*   *high*   *nice*   *expensive*   *big*
up-to-date   *wide*   *small*   *bad*   *easy*   *old*

	Adjective	Superlative
		+ *-est*
1	*fast*	*the fastest*
2		
3		
4		
		+ *-st*
5		
6		
		double consonant + *-est*
7		
		y + *-iest*
8		
9		
		most +
10		
11		
		irregular
12		
13		

3 Tick (✓) the correct sentence, a or b.

1 a That was the most important decision of my whole career.
   b That was most important decision in my whole career.

2 a I think Gina has the goodest marketing idea.
   b I think Gina has the best marketing idea.

3 a My mobile phone is the most up-to-date I could find.
   b My mobile phone is the most up-to-datest I could find.

4 a Our competitor is the bigest company in the market.
   b Our competitor is the biggest company in the market.

5 a That Internet provider is the most expensive, but offers the bestest service.
   b That Internet provider is the most expensive, but offers the best service.

6 a The German manufacturer makes the highest-quality goods in our field.
   b The German manufacturer makes the most highest-quality goods in our field.

Working with words

1 Match 1–6 to a–f to make phrases.

1 credit ___   a service
2 expiry ___   b call
3 room ___   c card
4 wake-up ___   d number
5 Internet ___   e date
6 card ___   f access

2 Complete the missing words in the conversation.

A Good evening. Do you have any ¹v_____?

B Yes. Would you like a ²s_____ or double room?

A Double, please.

B OK, we have a double room on the tenth ³f_____. It's 120 dollars and the price ⁴i_____ breakfast.

A That's fine, thanks. I'll take it.

B OK, do you have a credit card? We need one to ⁵b_____ the room.

A Of course. Here you are.

B Thanks. Please sign here. Here's your keycard. Is there anything else I can help you with?

A I need to get to the airport for 8.00 a.m. tomorrow morning. Can you order me a ⁶t_____?

B Of course. Which ⁷t_____ at the airport?

A Number 2.

B OK. The taxi will be here at 7.30 a.m.

A What time do you ⁸s_____ breakfast?

B From 6.00 a.m.

A Thanks.

B There are towels and a ⁹h_____ in the bathroom, and there's a ¹⁰s_____ in the wardrobe.

A Great, thanks. And where's the ¹¹l_____?

B It's just over there on the left.

A Thanks.

B Have a nice evening!

Business communication

1 ~~Cross out~~ the one incorrect response in 1–4.

1 A How was your meal?
   B *Very nice, thanks. / Very delicious. / Delicious, thanks.*

2 A Could I have the bill, please?
   B *Sounds good. / Certainly. / Sure.*

3 A Would you like a dessert?
   B *No, thanks. / Yes, please. / No, I don't.*

4 A Do you like sushi?
   B *Yes, I do. / Yes, please. / Yes, I love it.*

2 Complete the conversation with the correct words.

A Hello. Are you ¹_____ to ²_____?

B Yes, thanks. I'³_____ have the spaghetti bolognese, please.

C Mmm. The steak ⁴_____ good. I'⁵_____ like the steak and fries, please.

A ⁶_____ you like any side dishes?

B Do you ⁷_____ any salads?

A Yes, we have a green salad.

B OK, I'll ⁸_____ one of those, please.

C And ⁹_____ we have two colas, please?

A ¹⁰_____.

...

B ¹¹_____ me?

A Yes?

B Could I have the ¹²_____, please.

A Of ¹³_____. One ¹⁴_____, please.

3 Put the conversations in the correct order.

1

a ___ Would you like a side dish with that?

b ___ Yes, I'll have a four seasons pizza, please.

c ___ Are you ready to order?

d ___ No problem.

e ___ No, thanks, but I'd like a glass of mineral water, please.

2

a ___ How was your meal?

b ___ Would you like a dessert?

c ___ And could we have the bill, please?

d ___ Sure.

e ___ No, thank you, but we'd like two coffees, please.

f ___ Very nice, thanks.

Language at work

GRAMMAR REFERENCE

Going to

Form

Positive: Subject + *am/is/are* + *going to* + verb

I *am/'m going to* visit the new customer.
He *is/'s going to* write the next presentation.
They *are/'re going to* work in Brazil.

Negative: Subject + *am / is / are not* + *going to* + verb

I *am not / 'm not going to* take the job.
She *is not / isn't going to* leave the company.
We *are not / aren't going to* have a meeting about this.

Questions: (Question word) + *am/is/are* + subject + *going to* + verb?

Am I going to come to the meeting?
Why is he going to talk to management?
Are you going to visit the suppliers?

Short answers: Don't repeat *going to*.

A *Is he going to talk to management?*   B *No, he isn't.*
A *Are you going to visit the suppliers?*   B *Yes, I am.*

Use

To talk about a general plan for a future action or event.

It is used to mean the same as *I am planning to …*
There is not necessarily a fixed time in the plan.

I'm *going to visit* Toronto.
We *aren't going to eat* out in the evening.
Are you going to take Friday off?

Infinitive of purpose

Add an infinitive to say *why* you are doing something.

We're going to meet our suppliers **to discuss** prices.
They're going to spend a day in New York **to find** a new office.
I'm going to leave the office at 3.00 p.m. **to collect** my wife from the airport.

1 Make sentences from the prompts using *going to*.

1 They / visit / their customers.

_____

2 I / not / ask / Patrice to help.

_____

3 We / take / Tuesday off.

_____

4 It / not / rain today.

_____

5 you / discuss / the contract at the meeting?

_____

6 I / see / José at the conference.

_____

2 Match 1–6 to a–f to make sentences.

1 Franz is going to meet us at the airport before we leave ___
2 We're going to arrive early at check-in ___
3 Samir is going to come to the airport ___
4 Jake is going to attend the conference ___
5 We're going to work late ___
6 I'm going to contact our suppliers ___

a to find some new customers.
b to take us to our hotel.
c to miss the queues.
d to give us our visas.
e to ask about the order.
f to finish the presentation.

3 Correct the mistakes in 1–8.

1 The airline is going cancel its flights.

_____

2 Silvia going to attend the meeting instead of me.

_____

3 Marco are going to confirm his flight details tomorrow.

_____

4 I'm going to not finish the report by tomorrow.

_____

5 Are you visit Jess while you're in New York?

_____

6 Timo's going to call the suppliers for to cancel the order.

_____

7 Are you going to hold a meeting to discussing the IT problems?

_____

8 Franz isn't going take the new job.

_____

Working with words

1 Cross out the word in 1–6 that doesn't match the noun in **bold**.

1 tight / busy / fast   **schedule**
2 busy / annual / quiet   **period**
3 public / time / annual   **holiday**
4 tight / busy   **deadline**
5 annual / time   **off**
6 public / annual   **leave**

2 Klaus works for Pioneering, a seed company. He's talking about his job. Replace the phrases in **bold** with the phrases from the list.

annual leave   deadline   long weekend   public holiday
some time off   busy period

We have a **lot of work** [1]_____
at the beginning of the year. The shops need the seeds in February and our **final date**
[2]_____ to get the seeds ready is the end of January. It doesn't give us much time. I try to take **a break** [3]_____
at Easter, and in May we have a **national day off**
[4]_____, so I usually take a **holiday from Friday to Monday**
[5]_____. In the summer the company closes for two weeks and we all have our **holidays** [6]_____.

3 Complete the email with the words from the list.

timetable   annual conference   busy schedules
quiet period   tight   reminder

Subject: Next week

Dear Julio,

Thanks for the [1]_____
about my presentation at next week's
[2]_____. Unfortunately,
my [3]_____ now looks
very busy with the preparation for my
presentation, and I am worried about
the [4]_____ deadline
for the sales report. I know we all have
[5]_____ at the moment,
but I wanted to ask if I could give you the
report a week late. The week after next is
going to be a [6]_____ for
me, so I will have time to do it.

Thanks,

Paulo

Business communication

1 Put the words in *italics* in the correct order to complete the conversation.

A We have a few problems. *The / that / is / situation*
[1]_____ the ordering system has crashed.

B OK, we have a back-up and the technicians are working to fix it. *The / to / is / aim*
[2]_____ be working by lunchtime.

A Well, we need to hurry.

B Why? *What / deadline / 's / the*
[3]_____?

A The courier arrives at 1.00 p.m. to collect the goods, so *why / we / don't*
[4]_____ finish the orders we're working on? New orders will have to wait. I'll put a notice on the website to inform customers.

B Good idea. *So / summarize / to*
[5]_____, the current orders are OK, but new orders aren't. Is that right?

2 Complete the conversation with the expressions from the list.

How much time do we need for   Let's
I'm going to   We've already

A [1]_____ spent two days on the presentation and the meeting is tomorrow.

B [2]_____ the graphs and figures?

A Well, I'm waiting for Alexi to send them to me.

B [3]_____ call him and give him a deadline.

A OK. Can you do that?

B Sure, so you're going to finish as much as you can and [4]_____ call Alexi. OK?

3 Complete the expressions and find the hidden word.

1 The _ _ _ _ | _ | _ _ _ is two weeks behind.
2 What _ _ _ | _ | is the meeting?
3 The | _ | _ _ is to sign the contract by March.
4 Why | _ | _ _ _ we call the customer?
5 We _ | _ | _ _ to finish on Friday.
6 The _ | _ | _ _ _ _ _ _ is that the goods are late.
7 How long do we | _ | _ _ _ for the delivery?
8 Is _ _ | _ | _ _ _ _ _ happy with that date?
9 So, to | _ | _ _ _ _ _ _ _, we call John and …

Language at work

GRAMMAR REFERENCE

Present perfect

Form

Positive: Subject + *have/has* + past participle*

*I **have ordered** some more office paper.*

*He **has sent** the invoice to the wrong person.*

Negative: Subject + *have/has not* + past participle*

*We **have not received** your payment.*

*She **hasn't been** to Nepal.*

Questions: (Question word) + *have/has* + subject + past participle*

***Have you contacted** the suppliers?*

*Why **has he gone** to Canada?*

Short answers: Don't repeat the past participle*

A *Have you contacted the suppliers?*

B *Yes, I **have.***

*past participle

For regular verbs, add *-ed* to the verb, as for the rules for forming the past simple (see **Practice file 5** on page 95).

Use

To talk about an action in the past that has an effect on the present.

I have finished the report and given it to my boss.

Action in the past = finish the report, give it to my boss

Effect on the present = the report is on my boss's desk

Never use the present perfect to talk about an event in the past with a time expression (see **Practice file 6** on page 97 for time expressions).

---

1 Read the list of tasks then complete the email, saying what you have (✓) and haven't (✗) done.

> * Finish the report for Ajax. ✓
> * Call our suppliers. ✗
> * Finalize the menu for the buffet reception. ✓
> * Book hotel rooms for our Thai guests. ✓
> * Send the timetable of the visit to the guests. ✗
> * Check Irena's emails. ✓
> * Cancel Irena's flight to Sweden. ✗

Dear Irena,

I have been very busy, so I haven't done everything you asked.

- I ¹_____ the report for Ajax.
- I ²_____ our suppliers.
- I ³_____ the menu for the buffet reception.
- I ⁴_____ hotel rooms for our Thai guests.
- I ⁵_____ the timetable of the visit to the guests.
- I ⁶_____ your emails.
- I ⁷_____ your flight to Sweden.

Regards

2 Complete the conversation with the present perfect form of the verbs in brackets.

A ¹_____ (you / send) the order yet?

B No, I ²_____ (have / not).

A Why not? I ³_____ (post) them the invoice already!

B The order's not ready. The Production Department ⁴_____ (have) some problems.

A Oh, I ⁵_____ (not / speak) to Jeff from Production today, so no one told me.

B The packing machine ⁶_____ (break down) and they ⁷_____ (not / fix) it yet.

A OK, I'll call the customers and explain.

3 Correct the mistakes in 1–6.

1 They haven't the order completed.

_____

2 A Have you done the holiday timetable yet?

B Yes, I done. _____

3 Mikhail haven't replied yet.

_____

4 A Do they have confirmed the hotel booking?

B No, they haven't. _____

5 I've work in IT development and on the helpdesk.

_____

6 Thiery's took the last car from our car pool.

_____

Communication activities

Unit 1 | Language at work, Exercise 8

Student A

Ask and answer questions about the people below. Use some of the information from the list to complete their profiles.

Germany   IT companies   TUX   Managing Director
restaurants   Brazil   Spain   Receptionist
supermarkets   Excel

Example: *Is Renate from Germany?*

1

NAME Renate
COUNTRY _____
COMPANY NAME _____
JOB *Sales Director*
CUSTOMERS *small businesses*

2

NAME Eiji
COUNTRY *Japan*
COMPANY NAME *Takeyama*
JOB _____
CUSTOMERS _____

3

NAMES Ramiro and Carmen
COUNTRY _____
COMPANY NAME *Sema*
JOB *Sales Reps*
CUSTOMERS _____

Unit 3 | Practically speaking, Exercise 5

Student A

Ask Student B questions to complete their contact details.

Student A	Student B
Pacific Exports Head Office	
62 Bay Rd	
Wellington	
New Zealand	
6011	
dani_jones@nznet.co.nz	

Unit 2 | Talking point, Task

Student A

Company: _____
Produces: *trains and trams*
Nationality: _____
Head office: _____
Number of employees: _____
Exports to: _____

1 The paper company is Japanese.
2 The company with its head office in Tokyo has 13,000 employees.
3 The fruit company's head office is in Cape Town.
4 Chrysler exports cars to Europe, China, Mexico and Canada.

Unit 3 | Business communication, Exercise 7

Student A

1 You want to order some satnavs for your company. Call your supplier, Student B. Use this information to make your order.

   Your company: FR Logistics

   Your company address: 26 Mill Road, Durban, South Africa, 4091

   Your email address: yourname@frlogistics.co.za

   You want to order: 15 satnavs

   Product code: 282BN

   You want:
   • delivery as soon as possible
   • to pay by credit card
   • the supplier to confirm your order by email

2 You work for a supplier of kitchen products. Student B calls you. Use this information to take their order.

   Product CF72 is in stock. Customers can pay by credit card. Delivery is free.

   You want:
   • the customer's email address
   • the delivery address

Unit 10 | Practically speaking, Exercise 4

Student B

Here is your news. Tell your partner.
1 Your favourite colleague is leaving the company.
2 Your company won a new contract yesterday.
3 No one's receiving a pay rise this year.

Unit 3 | Talking point, Task

Student A

Vienna, Austria	
Location	In the centre of Europe.
Transport to the city	Seventy airlines to 180 destinations in over 60 countries. Road and railway connections to Central European countries.
Transport in the city	Sixteen minutes from airport to city centre by train. Fast public transport. Small city centre – good for walking.
Conference facilities	Three conference centres, e.g. Austria Centre Vienna with 180 meeting rooms for 10 to 4,320 people. 85 conference hotels.
Cost	High

Vancouver, Canada	
Location	
Transport to the city	
Transport in the city	
Conference facilities	
Cost	

Unit 5 | Language at work, Exercise 4

Student A

1 You weren't at a presentation last week. Your partner was. Check if the report below is correct.
   Example: Was the presentation on Tuesday morning?

> **Presentation:** Future plans
>
> **Time:** Tuesday morning (?)
>
> **Present:** Jan, Lydia, Janusz, Carlos (?)
>
> **Venue:** The conference room (?)
>
> **Speaker:** Managing Director (?)

2 Now answer your partner's questions about this report.

> **Presentation:** Profits for this year
>
> **Time:** Wednesday morning
>
> **Present:** Jan, Lydia, Janusz, Carlos, Piotr
>
> **Venue:** The conference room
>
> **Speaker:** Financial Director

Unit 5 | Working with words, Exercise 9

Student A

1 You are away on a business trip. Student B has two emails for you and calls you for help. Ask what the emails are about and give the following instructions:
   • Email 1: Reply and attach electronic copy. It's in the folder marked 'Newbroch'.
   • Email 2: Forward it to HR and reply to the applicant.
2 Student B is on a training course. You check his or her email. Call Student B and explain the emails. Ask what to do. Make notes and check you understand.

>
>
> Can you send me a copy of the Finance report? Thanks.
>
> Gill

>
>
> With reference to our order (see attached) for 20 of item P-166, we only have 10 boxes. Where are the other 10 boxes?
>
> Felicia Hildebrandt

Unit 5 | Language at work, Exercise 8

Student A

1 You received this message. Ask your partner for the missing information. Use the question words in brackets.

> Mr Simons called at _____ a.m. (When …?)
>
> He called about _____. (What …?)
>
> He didn't come to the meeting because
> _____. (Why …?)
>
> He wanted to know _____ of the next
> conference. (What …?)
>
> Please call him back if you want him to speak at the
> conference.

2 Now answer your partner's questions about the information in this phone message.

> From: Mr Koch
>
> Time: 2.00 p.m.
>
> Subject: Trip to Germany last week.
>
> Message: Hans was sick – another meeting next
> month.

Unit 5 | Business communication, Exercise 4

Student A

Read more information about the problems in the email.
- Astrid, the receptionist, is sick today.
- You called IT about the printers, but no one answered.
- You didn't remember to book the tickets.
- You can buy Ellen a leaving present.

Now call your partner.
1 Explain and solve the problems together.
2 Promise action.

Unit 12 | Business communication, Exercise 4

Student C

You are responsible for printing and postage.
The printers need about three weeks.
You think it's going to take about two weeks to send the brochures out to customers.
You have annual leave between 10th October and 17th October.
Discuss the final schedule and write down the stages with all the important dates.

Unit 6 | Practically speaking, Exercise 4

Student A

1 Look at these pictures and answer your partner's questions about this trip.

2 Now ask your partner questions 1–5 about his/her trip.
1 How was the journey?
2 How was the hotel?
3 How was the food?
4 How was the meeting?
5 How was the city?

Unit 12 | Language at work, Exercise 7

Student B

Here is a list of your tasks for the week. Ask Student A if he/she has done his/her tasks and say if you have done yours.

Example: Have you ordered a new computer?

You	Done?	Student A
book venue for annual conference?	no	order a new computer?
write minutes for team meeting?	no	ship delivery to Argentina?
organize meeting with union rep?	yes	call clients about new product?
ask boss for some time off?	no	email new brochure to clients?

Unit 7 | Language at work, Exercise 3

Student A

1 Describe this company plan to Student B.
   Example: The cafeteria is below Sales and Marketing.

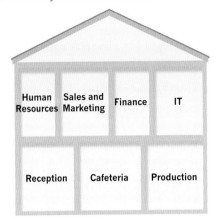

2 Listen to Student B. Write in the rooms and departments.

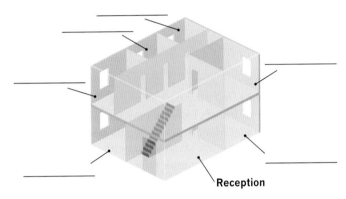

Reception

Unit 5 | Working with words, Exercise 9

Student B

1 Student A is away on a business trip. You check his or
   her email. Call Student A and explain the emails. Ask
   what to do. Make notes and check you understand.

> ✉
>
> Can I have an order form and a copy of this
> year's brochure?
>
> Thanks,
>
> Jiri
> Hanron Solutions

> ✉
>
> Dear Sir or Madam,
>
> Further to your advert for a trainee sales
> person, please find attached a copy of my CV.

2 You are on a training course. Student A checks your
   email and calls you for help. Ask what the emails are
   about and give the following instructions.
   • Email 1: It's in a folder called 'Budgets'. Please print her
     a hard copy.
   • Email 2: Forward it to the right department – it's not my
     responsibility.

Unit 6 | Business communication, Exercise 7

Student A

Role-play these situations.

1 It's the first morning of an annual conference. It's your
   first time at the conference. The first session is in Room
   125, but where is it? Student B speaks to you.

2 You are in Reception at your company. A visitor wants
   to see Sara Olsen, who is on the third floor. Speak to
   him/her.

Unit 7 | Business communication, Exercise 3

Student A

1 Call your partner and check these details.
   | | |
   Ms Bebiyon   Tel. 07 364 330?
   Mr Gibuvo   Tel. 0034 711 5400?
2 Your partner calls to check these details.
   Mr Kassabygy   Tel. 0041 909 5520
   Ms Herrera   Tel. 0709 553 627

Unit 7 | Business communication, Exercise 6

Student A

Call 1

You are Megumi Yoshida. Call Michelle McGoldrick about
your hotel reservation. You want the hotel details as soon
as possible. Your phone number is 078 546 2394.

Call 2

You are Youssuf Hussein's assistant. He is at lunch.
Answer the phone and take a message.

Message for:	
From:	
Phone number:	
Calling about:	
Please call back:	Urgent:

Unit 12 | Business communication, Exercise 4

Student B

You are responsible for information and design for the
brochure.

You think it's going to take about six weeks to get all the
information. The designers need about four weeks. You
have annual leave between 15th August and 30th August.
Discuss the final schedule and write down the stages with
all the important dates.

Unit 8 | Business communication, Exercise 6

Student A

You are Chen. Here's your calendar on Thursday.

Thursday

09.00–10.00	Visit factory
10.00–11.00	Return at 11.10
11.00–12.00	
12.00–14.00	
12.10–13.10	Lunch with Ania

Unit 9 | Business communication, Exercise 6

Student A

You and your partner need to choose a new courier company for important deliveries, and a hotel for some two-day training seminars around the country.

- You have quotes from two courier firms.
- Your partner has quotes from two hotels.
- Take turns to ask and tell each other about the quotes, and then make a choice together.

Company: Speed Merchants

Price: €10 per kilometre

Online tracking: Uses up-to-date satellite technology to find a fast route. You can check the location of your package online.

Location: Centres in over 20 cities.

– very friendly staff on the phone

– no discounts

Company: Go Fast

Price: €9.95 per kilometre

Guaranteed delivery: Money back if late.

Location: Centres in 18 cities.

– staff were slow to answer the phone

– no way to check location of packages online

– offered free delivery for every ten deliveries

Unit 8 | Talking point, Stage 2

Student A

MONDAY	
09.00 doctor	
11.00–12.00 HR weekly meeting	
15.00–17.00 meeting with personnel agency	
TUESDAY	
13.00–14.00 lunch – out of office	
15.00–17.00 team meeting	
WEDNESDAY	
15.00–17.00 meeting with department heads	
THURSDAY	
14.00–leave work, take Jamie to dentist	
FRIDAY	

Unit 10 | Practically speaking, Exercise 4

Student A

Here is your news. Tell your partner.

1 Everyone in your team likes the new Team Leader.
2 Your Department Manager is having dinner with the new Human Resources Manager tonight!
3 The company is opening three new factories abroad.

Unit 11 | Working with words, Exercise 9

Student A

Now you are a visitor. Check in and ask for information on the following:

- wake-up call at 6.30 a.m.?
- restaurant in hotel? necessary to book?
- meeting room for tomorrow at 10.00 a.m.?
- sauna and solarium?

Unit 2 | Talking point, Task

Student D

Company: *Nippon Paper Industries*
Produces: _____
Nationality: _____
Head office: _____
Number of employees: _____
Exports to: _____

1 The train and tram company is Polish.
2 2,000 employees produce fruit.
3 Afrifresh is a South African company.
4 Pesa produces trains and trams.

Unit 11 | Talking point, Task

Travel information:

	Flights	Train	Car
Madrid–Paris / Paris–Madrid	21 flights/day, 2 hours, €80	10 hours, €110 return	11.5 hours
Madrid–Lisbon / Lisbon–Madrid	13 flights/day, 1 hour, 15 mins, €70	Overnight sleeper, €150 return	6 hours
Madrid–Lyon / Lyon–Madrid	2 flights/day, 1 hour, 45 mins, €80	20 hours, €150 return	10.5 hours
Lisbon–Lyon / Lyon–Lisbon	2 flights/day, 2 hours, 25 mins, €100	21 hours, €170 return	16 hours
Lisbon–Paris / Paris–Lisbon	14 flights/day, 2.5 hours, €90	Overnight sleeper, €200 return	16 hours
Paris–Lyon / Lyon–Paris	2 flights/day, 1 hour, 45 mins, €80	2 hours, €75 return	4.5 hours

Accommodation information:

	Average business hotel	Average Airbnb
Lisbon	€130	€90
Lyon	€170	€90
Paris	€200	€120

All prices and times are approximate.

Unit 12 | Language at work, Exercise 7

Student A

Here is a list of your tasks for the week. Ask Student B if he/she has done his/her tasks and say if you have done yours.

> **Example:** *Have you booked a venue for the annual conference?*

You	Done?	Student B
order a new computer?	yes	book venue for annual conference?
ship delivery to Argentina?	no	write minutes for team meeting?
call clients about new product?	no	organize meeting with union rep?
email new brochure to clients?	yes	ask boss for some time off?

Unit 12 | Business communication, Exercise 4

Student A

You are responsible for the schedule. You need to schedule the following stages:

- product details and price list
- design
- printing
- sending the brochures to customers

Find out from Students B and C how long each stage takes. You want to send the brochure to clients by 1st November at the latest. Also find out when Students B and C have time off because this will change the schedule.

Discuss the final schedule and write down the stages with all the important dates.

Unit 1 | Language at work, Exercise 8

Student B

Ask and answer questions about the people below. Use some of the information from the list to complete their profiles.

Japan   India   Sema   small businesses   Sales Reps
Takeyama   multinationals   Sales Director
Personal Assistant   Uchida

> **Example:** *Is Renate a Sales Director?*

1

NAME Renate
COUNTRY *Germany*
COMPANY NAME *TUX*
JOB _____
CUSTOMERS _____

2

NAME Eiji
COUNTRY _____
COMPANY NAME _____
JOB *Managing Director*
CUSTOMERS *IT companies*

3

NAMES Ramiro and Carmen
COUNTRY *Brazil*
COMPANY NAME _____
JOB _____
CUSTOMERS *supermarkets*

Unit 2 | Talking point, Task

Student B

Company: _____
Produces: _____
Nationality: _____
Head office: _____
Number of employees: _____
Exports to: _54 countries_

1 The American company produces cars.
2 The Polish company's head office is in Bydgoszcz.
3 78,000 employees work for the company with its head office in Michigan.
4 3,700 employees work for Pesa.

Unit 3 | Language at work, Exercise 5

Student B

You work at The Dubai Grand Hotel. Use the information below to help you answer Student A's questions about the hotel.

> **Example:** A Is there a bus to the airport?
>   B Yes, there's a bus every 20 minutes.

The Dubai Grand Hotel

• Buses to airport every 20 minutes.
• Car park for 100 cars.
• No restaurant in the hotel. There are some international restaurants near the hotel.
• Swimming pool and gym.
• Internet access in all rooms.
• Bank and post service in hotel.
• Six meeting rooms.
• The hotel has a free taxi service to city centre.

Unit 3 | Language at work, Exercise 4

Student A

You work at The Arabian Garden Hotel. Use the information below to help you answer Student B's questions about the hotel.

> **Example:** B Is there a bus to the airport?
>   A Yes, there's a bus every 30 minutes and there are also buses to the city centre.

The Arabian Garden Hotel

• Bus to airport every 30 minutes and to city centre every 15 minutes.
• No car park, but guests can park on the street. There is also car hire at Reception.
• Two restaurants and one bar.
• Swimming pool, gym and sauna.
• Internet access in all rooms.
• Conference room for 80 people and four meeting rooms.
• The hotel has a tourist information service and there are day trips to places of interest.

Unit 3 | Practically speaking, Exercise 5

Student B

Ask Student A questions to complete their contact details.

Student A	Student B
	HR dept, City Hotels
	49 Ardwick St
	Manchester
	UK
	M12 8BG
	ashley.smith@cityhotels.co.uk

Unit 3 | Business communication, Exercise 7

Student B

1 You work for a supplier of electronic products. Student A calls you. Use this information to take their order.
   Product 282BN is out of stock. You can deliver product 288BN tomorrow.
   Customers can pay by credit card.
   You want:
   • the customer's email address
   • the delivery address

2 You want to order some coffee machines for your company. Call your supplier, Student A. Use this information to make your order.
   Your company: Macquires
   Your email address: yourname@macquires.co.uk
   Your company address: 63 Farringdon Way, London, UK, W1 3AG
   You want to order: eight coffee machines
   Product code: CF72
   You want:
   • the supplier to confirm your order by email
   • to pay by credit card
   • free delivery

Unit 8 | Business communication, Exercise 5

Student B

You are Dolores. Here's your calendar on Thursday:

Thursday	
09.00–10.00	
10.00–11.00	
10.20–10.50	Conference call to Singapore.
11.00–12.00	
12.00–14.00	Meeting with Kasia and bank representative

Unit 3 | Talking point, Task

Student B

Vienna, Austria	
Location	
Transport to the city	
Transport in the city	
Conference facilities	
Cost	

Vancouver, Canada	
Location	North America.
Transport to the city	About 90 airlines. Direct flights to about 60 international destinations. Vancouver International Airport named 'Best Airport in North America'. Road and railway connections to Canadian and US cities.
Transport in the city	Thirty minutes from airport to city centre by train. Excellent public transport: bus, train, tram and boat.
Conference facilities	Five conference centres, e.g. Vancouver Convention and Exhibition centre with 2,300 m² of meeting space. More than 40 conference hotels.
Cost	Medium

Unit 9 | Business communication, Exercise 6

Student B

You and your partner need to choose a new courier company for important deliveries, and a hotel for some two-day training seminars around the country.

- You have quotes from two hotels.
- Your partner has quotes from two courier firms.
- Take turns to ask and tell each other about the quotes, and then make a choice together.

Hotels: InCountry

Price: €5,000 (for ten people)

Facilities: Many hotels provide secretarial service with fax, Internet, printers.

Locations: Over 35 hotels. Hotels are in the countryside, but easy to find.

Leisure: Most hotels have swimming pools and gym facilities.

– all hotels are different and restaurants serve local dishes

– friendly customer service person on the phone

Hotels: Vacationworld

Price: €5,100 (for 12 people)

Facilities: All hotels have two or more meeting rooms.

Locations: 30 hotels near or in city centres.

Leisure: Ten Vacationworld Plus hotels have swimming pools, sauna and gym.

– staff were polite and helpful

– all hotels are modern; restaurants serve wide range (Italian, Chinese, Indian, etc.)

Unit 2 | Talking point, Task

Student C

Company: _____

Produces: _____

Nationality: _American_

Head office: _____

Number of employees: _____

Exports to: _____

1 The South African company exports to 54 countries.
2 The European company exports to Europe, especially Germany.
3 They export paper and paper products worldwide.
4 Michigan is in the USA.

Unit 7 | Business communication, Exercise 3

Student B

1 Your partner calls to check these details.
  Ms Babayan   Tel. 077 364 3300
  Mr Jibowo   Tel. 0033 771 5440
2 Call your partner and check these details.
  Mr Kasebiggy Tel. 001 908 5220?
  Ms Hirrarer   Tel. 070 953 6227?

Unit 5 | Language at work, Exercise 4

Student B

1 Your partner wants to know if the report below is correct. You were at the presentation last week. Your partner wasn't. Answer his/her questions
  Example: Was the presentation on Tuesday morning?

  Presentation: Future plans

  Time: Tuesday morning

  Present: Jan, Lydia, Carlos

  Venue: Room 305

  Speaker: Managing Director

2 Now ask your partner questions about this report.

  Presentation: Profits for this year

  Time: Thursday morning (?)

  Present: Jan, Janusz, Lydia, Carlos (?)

  Venue: The conference room (?)

  Speaker: Managing Director and Financial Director (?)

Unit 11 | Working with words, Exercise 8

Student B

You are a visitor. Check in and ask for information on the following:
• dinner in room
• times for breakfast
• swimming pool
• Internet access in the hotel

Unit 5 | Language at work, Exercise 8

Student B

1 Answer your partner's questions about the information in this phone message.

  From: Mr Simons

  Time: 9.30 a.m.

  Subject: Next month's conference

  Message: In Canada. Date of next conference?

2 You received this message. Ask your partner for the missing information. Use the question words in brackets.

  Mr Koch called at _____ p.m. (When …?)

  He called about the _____ last week. (What …?)

  Hans cancelled the meeting because _____. (Why …?)

  We arranged another meeting for _____. (When …?)

  Please call him back.

Unit 5 | Business communication, Exercise 4

Student B

Read more information about the problems in the email.
• Your assistant is not very busy today.
• We emailed the wrong invoice. You'll contact them after the meeting.
• The IT department has a training course today and tomorrow.
• You booked a restaurant for Ellen's leaving party.
Now call your partner.
1 Explain and solve the problems together.
2 Promise action.

Unit 6 | Business communication, Exercise 7

Student B

Role-play these situations.
1 It's the first morning of a conference. You're one of the organizers. Room 125 is on the first floor. You think Student A has a problem. Speak to him/her.
2 You are a visitor at a company. It's your first time at the company. You are here to see Sara Olsen. Student A speaks to you.

Unit 8 | Talking point, Stage 2

Student B

MONDAY	Holiday
TUESDAY	11.30–13.30 meeting
WEDNESDAY	11.00–13.00 phone duty at Reception
THURSDAY	10.00–12.00 go to customers
FRIDAY	08.30 appointment at bank

Unit 7 | Language at work, Exercise 3

Student B

1 Listen to Student A. Write in the rooms and departments.

2 Describe this company plan to Student A.
Example: IT is behind Reception.

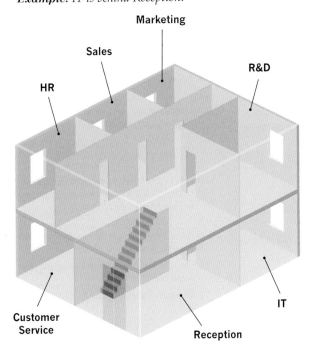

Unit 6 | Practically speaking, Exercise 4

Student B

1 Ask your partner these questions about his/her trip.
1 How was the journey?
2 How was the hotel?
3 How was the food?
4 How was the meeting?
5 How was the city?
2 Now look at these pictures and answer your partner's questions about this trip.

Unit 7 | Business communication, Exercise 6

Student B

Call 1

You work in an office with Michelle McGoldrick. She is out. Answer the phone and take a message.

Message for:	
From:	
Phone number:	
Calling about:	
Please call back:	Urgent:

Call 2

You are Henri Watunda. Call Youssuf Hussein about your meeting this evening. You are at The Arabian Garden Hotel in Dubai. Your room number is 701. The hotel number is 00971 4228663.

Audio scripts

Unit 1

1.1

Dahlia is Indian.
Raquel is Brazilian.
Randy is American.
Lukasz is Polish.
Tiziana is Italian.
Charlotte is British.
Yuko is Japanese.
Jacob is South African.

1.2

Japan	India
Japanese	American
British	Brazilian
Italy	Polish
Italian	Africa

1.3

1 I'm from India. I'm a receptionist for an American company.
2 Hello. I'm from Brazil. I'm a human resources manager. I work for an Italian company.
3 Hi. I'm a sales rep. I'm from the USA, but my company is Japanese.
4 Hello. I'm Polish and I'm a team leader for an Indian company.
5 Hi. I'm a personal assistant from Italy. I work for a Polish company.
6 Hello. I'm the Chief Executive Officer for a British company and I'm from the UK.
7 Hello. I'm Japanese. I'm a technician for a Brazilian company.
8 I'm a financial director from South Africa. I work for a South African company.

1.4

A So, is Marcegaglia a family company?
B Yes, it is. Steno Marcegaglia started the company in 1959, and his children Antonio and Emma are the CEOs.
A Are they from a big family?
B No, they're from a small family, but Marcegaglia isn't a small company. It's a multi-billion euro company with 7,000 employees.
A And are all the employees in Italy?
B They are in Italy and in many other countries, too, such as Brazil and China.

1.5

1 A H J K
2 B C D E G P T V (Z)
3 F L M N S X (Z)
4 I Y
5 O
6 Q U W
7 R

1.6

1
A What's his name?
B Mr Gorski.
A How do you spell that?
B G-O-R-S-K-I.
A Thanks.

2
A What's your company?
B Lufthansa.
A How do you spell that?
B L-U-F-T-H-A-N-S-A.
A Thanks.

1.7

Alek Hello. My name is Alek Gorski. That's G-O-R-S-K-I. We have an appointment with Mrs Da Rocha.
Eva How do you do, Mr Gorski? I'm Eva, Maria Da Rocha's assistant.
Alek Pleased to meet you, Eva. This is my assistant, Elzbieta Wozniak.
Eva Nice to meet you, Elzbieta. Sorry – how do you spell that?
Elzbieta Elzbieta? That's E-L-Z-B-I-E-T-A.
Eva E-L-Z-B-I-E-T-A. Thanks. Just a moment. Maria, your visitors are here …
Maria … Alek. It's good to see you again.
Alek And you. How are you?
Maria I'm fine. And you?
Alek Not so bad. Maria, do you know Elzbieta? She's my new assistant.
Maria No. How do you do, Elzbieta?
Elzbieta Pleased to meet you.

1.8

Maria See you soon, Alek.
Alek Yes, goodbye, Maria.
Maria Nice meeting you, Elzbieta.
Elzbieta Nice meeting you, too.
Maria Bye. Have a good journey.
Alek Thanks. Bye.

Unit 2

2.1

William Nice to see you again, Natasha. Do you know Malik?
Natasha No. Hello, I'm Natasha Darcy. Nice to meet you.
Malik You, too. Where do you work?
Natasha I'm with Perfect Match. It's a small recruitment company. We provide staff – especially in the pharmaceuticals industry. What about you?
Malik I work for a company called RiskLink. We produce software for financial services companies.
Natasha Oh right. What about you, William? Do you still work in electronics?
William Well, yes, but I don't have a job right now. That's why I'm here. I want to find something in the automobile industry, if possible.

2.2

pharmaceuticals	hotel
electronics	finance
recruitment	automobile

2.3

Kikkoman is a Japanese company and we sell 400 million litres of soy sauce every year. We employ around 6,000 people in total. We export soy sauce all over the world, including Asia, North America, Australia and Europe. We also develop new products for the pharmaceuticals industry. Restaurants, supermarkets and Asian food shops buy our products and we also provide lessons in Japanese cooking – using Kikkoman products, of course!

2.4

A Our first business area is Food and Food Service. We produce sugar and cooking oil. The company has restaurants, cafés and food shops. It provides meals for restaurants, schools and hospitals. Our second business area is Bio Pharma. Here we produce pharmaceuticals and medicines.
B And do you export these products?
A Yes, we do. We export medicines to countries around the world. And we develop new biotechnological products. The third area, Entertainment and Media, is now the main business of CJ. The company produces films for the Korean market and abroad.
B Does the company import films, too?
A Yes, it does. We import films from foreign production companies like DreamWorks, and we have eight cable TV channels in Korea and a chain of cinemas. The fourth business area is Home Shopping and Logistics. We provide a home shopping service for customers, 24 hours a day.
B Do customers buy on the Internet?
A Yes, they do, but also on satellite TV. We have a logistics centre. It provides transport and delivery services.

2.5

1
A Do you export these products?
B Yes, we do.
2
A Does the company import films, too?
B Yes, it does.
3
A Does CJ provide financial services?
B No, it doesn't provide financial services.
4
A Do you import medicines?
B No, we don't. We export medicines.

2.6

1
A Can I have your phone number?
B Certainly. It's oh seven seven eight, four five six, three six five.
2
A What's the price for that mobile phone?
B It's $45.60.
3 One thousand three hundred employees work here.
4 We started the company in 2001.

2.7

1

Receptionist Good morning. TE Media.

Anna Good morning. This is Anna Lillis from OPT Bank. Is Peter Bawden there, please?

Receptionist Yes, I'll put you through.

Anna Thanks …

Peter … Hello. Peter Bawden speaking.

Anna Hi, Peter. It's Anna Lillis.

Peter Hi, Anna.

Anna I'm calling about your email …

Anna … So that's eleven o'clock.

Peter That's right.

Anna OK, see you soon.

Peter See you. Bye.

2

Receptionist Hello. The Dubai Grand Hotel. How can I help you?

Sadler Hello. This is Raymond Sadler from Sadler Business Services. I'm calling about your meeting rooms …

Receptionist … and there's Internet access in each room.

Sadler That's great. Thanks for your help.

Receptionist You're welcome.

Sadler Goodbye.

Receptionist Goodbye.

Unit 3

3.1

Good afternoon. I'd like to tell you about the LEGO group. They are a family company with their head office in Billund, in Denmark, but they operate in many countries. In Billund, they also have their research and development centre and a factory. They have two more factories in Europe: in the Czech Republic and Hungary. In Asia, they have one factory in China, and in North America, they have one factory in Mexico. They have sales offices worldwide: around 20 in Europe, around ten in Asia, four in North America, one in South America, two in Australia and one in Africa. They have two large distribution centres in the Czech Republic and in the USA. Of course, there are LEGO shops all over the world. And online, their website, LEGO.com, has 21 local sites for LEGO fans in different countries.

3.2

A Dubai is a great location for a conference. The weather is always good.

B What about the airport? Are there lots of international flights?

A Yes, there are. And there isn't a problem with transport from the airport because public transport is excellent in Dubai.

B But is there a good place for a conference?

A Yes, there is. It's the Dubai International Exhibition and Convention complex. It's perfect.

3.3

1 My email address is Peter dot Tieng at Forresters dot CA.

2 Her email address is Alina underscore DL at G-mail dot com.

3 Our email address is jobs hyphen info at top communications, all one word, dot co dot UK.

4 Their mailing address is Accounts Department, Blair and Browns, 99 Edward Street, Toronto, M5V 2MD.

5 His postal address is 21 Old School Road, Glasgow, and the postcode is G21 4YU.

6 The company address is seven-four-two Quaker Street, Seattle, and the zip code is nine-eight-one-zero-four.

3.4

A Can you give me your address, please?

B Yes, it's 30 Grosvenor Street, Cambridge.

A Is that *30* Grosvenor Street?

B Yes, that's right.

A And can you spell Grosvenor for me?

B Of course. It's G-R-O-S-V-E-N-O-R.

A Thanks. And what's the postcode, please?

B CB7 9BT.

A CB7 9TB.

B No, it's 9BT, not 9TB.

A Oh, right. So that's CB7 9BT. Got it. And what's your email address, please?

B It's Chris dot Oakley at homenet dot co dot UK.

A Sorry, can you repeat that, please?

B Sure. Chris dot Oakley – that's O-A-K-L-E-Y – at homenet dot co dot UK.

A Thanks very much.

3.5

A Hello. Workspace Supplies. How can I help you?

B Hello. This is Dan Kashani from York Services. Can I order some whiteboards, please?

A Yes, of course. Can you tell me the product code?

B Yes, it's 9082WB. Can I order three, please?

A 9082WB … I'm sorry, but that product is out of stock. We have another whiteboard, the 9099WB. It's the same price.

B €92?

A Yes, that's right. So that's €276 in total for three.

B OK. Thanks. And can I check the delivery time, please? Is it next-day delivery?

A That's right. We can deliver them tomorrow. Can I have your delivery address?

B Sure. It's 24B Portland Street, Manchester, M1 5WD.

A Sorry, can you repeat the postcode, please?

B Yes, M1 5WD. And can you confirm my order by email, please?

A Yes. What's your email address, please?

B It's Dan dot Kashani at york services, all one word, dot co dot UK.

A Sorry, can you say that more slowly?

B Dan dot Kashani at york services, all one word, dot co dot UK.

A Got it. Thanks for your order.

B Thanks for your help. Goodbye.

A Goodbye.

Unit 4

4.1

A So, how do you use *Paym*?

B It's easy. Open your bank's mobile banking app or online banking website. Log in with your username and password. Then press the *Paym* button, or click on the *Paym* link if you are using your laptop. On the next screen you can enter the details, for example, the amount of money you want to send. It's a bit like sending a text message.

A I see.

B First, if you have more than one account, select the account you want to send the money from. Then select someone from your contact list or key in a mobile number. Next, enter the amount and press 'pay now'.

A That does sound easy.

B Yes. And the other person gets the money in their account seconds later, and they receive confirmation of that by SMS message.

A You mean text message?

B That's right.

A Sounds good. And can I pay anyone?

B No, if you want to send or receive money with *Paym*, all users need to register for the service first. This links your bank account with your mobile phone number. So you need to register first, too. We can do it now. Are you logged in to your mobile banking account?

A Yes, but I need to charge my phone first. The battery is low.

B OK. There's a power point over here.

A Thanks. I'll just log out first.

4.2

1 Log in to your account with your username and password.

2 Press the *Paym* button or click on the *Paym* link if you are using your laptop.

3 On the next screen you can enter the details.

4 It's a bit like sending a text message.

5 Select someone from your contact list.

6 **A** I need to charge my phone first. The battery is low.

  B OK. There's a power point over here.

4.3

First of all, the warehouse computer receives customer orders. Then, the computer tells a robot to find the correct box. Next, the robot finds the box and delivers it to a human co-worker. After that, the person takes the correct items for the order. And finally, the robot returns the box and starts again.

4.4

Nathan Why doesn't it work?!

Melissa Can I help, Nathan?

Nathan That would be great, thanks. I want to log in to the file-sharing system, but the password doesn't work. I have it here. Can you help me?

Melissa Sure. The password is all in lower-case letters. Don't use upper-case letters.

Nathan Oh! I see. I'm in now – thanks very much.

Melissa You're welcome.

Nathan But … where's the meetings folder?

Melissa Do you want a hand again?

Nathan Yes, please. Josh says the next meeting notes are in the meetings folder, but I can't see a meetings folder.

Melissa Let's have a look. Hmm … No, I can't see it either. You can search for it.

Nathan How do I do that?

Melissa There's a search box in the top right-hand corner. Write the folder name in there.

Nathan OK, thanks. No, nothing. I still can't find it.

Melissa Hmm. Maybe the folder isn't shared. You need to accept an email invitation to share the folder first.

Nathan Oh, do I? I don't know how to do that. Can you give me a hand again?

Melissa Yes, of course. Is there an email invitation from Josh in your inbox?

Nathan Just a minute – I'll have a look. Oh yes, here it is!

Melissa Now, just click on 'view folder' in the email.

Nathan Ah, here it is. Great! Thanks very much, Melissa.

Melissa You're welcome.

4.5

1 In all our supermarkets this technology saves us money, and it is fast and easy for our customers to pay for their shopping.

2 I like to check my emails and read the news when I go to work on the train in the morning.

3 I'm a hairdresser. This is useful for me to speak to customers on the phone at the same time as when I'm cutting a customer's hair.

4 I like this because it helps me to do enough exercise – I can see how much I walk and run every day.

5 This is good for our delivery company because our drivers can easily find the right address when they deliver packages.

6 I like it because there are some good apps on it and I can choose when to watch my favourite TV programmes on the big screen.

Unit 5

5.1

A Hi, Michelle. It's Rona.

B Oh, hello. How can I help?

A Well, Hanran Solutions telephoned. They received our invoice for an order of scanners, but they say it's wrong. Did you print a hard copy of the original order form?

B No, but I always save their order forms. Let me open the folder. What was the date on it?

A The third of May.

B That's strange. It isn't here. Sorry about that. One moment. Did they attach the document to an email?

A Yes. I think they sent the email on the third.

B OK, here's an email from Hanran Solutions on the third with an attachment.

A That sounds good.

B Yes, it's an order for 20 scanners.

A Great. Can you forward the email to me?

B Sure.

5.2

Janusz Sorry I'm late. I was at the presentation on branding.

Carlos Oh, was that this morning?

Janusz Yes, at 7.30 in the Century Hotel.

Carlos Oh. Was it good?

Janusz Yes, the presentation was really interesting and there were lots of good questions at the end.

Carlos Were there many people there?

Janusz There weren't many people for the breakfast at the start, but there were lots for the presentation. It was too early for some people!

Carlos Were *you* on time?

Janusz Of course! But the breakfast wasn't very good. Anyway, why weren't you in the office yesterday?

Carlos There were terrible problems with my flight back from Rome, so I …

5.3

Piotr Hello?

Lydia Hi, Piotr. It's Lydia. Sorry I missed your call.

Piotr No problem. I wanted to ask about the event. Did you call Ron Peters?

Lydia Yes, I did. I called him yesterday. He can do the presentation, but not in the morning. He's busy then.

Piotr OK, so what time did you decide to start?

Lydia 12.30, so it will be a lunch meeting. I invited him to have lunch with us.

Piotr Good. And did you book the hotel?

Lydia No, I didn't. I phoned the Century Hotel, but they don't have any free rooms at lunchtime. The Parade Hotel has a meeting room free, but I didn't book it because I didn't know if it was OK for you.

Piotr Yes, the Parade Hotel is fine, thanks.

Lydia OK, I'll call them now.

Piotr Great. Thanks, Lydia.

5.4

1

A Hello. Sorry I'm late. My train was very late.

B That's OK. We called you, but you didn't answer.

A Yes, sorry. I wanted to call you, too, but my battery is low.

B No problem. We can start now …

2

A Now, about the team-building weekend, we decided to ask the Century and the Princess Hotels. Did you call them about prices?

B No, I didn't. Sorry about that. I was really busy yesterday because we had visitors all day. I'll do it this morning.

3

A Great work on the training last week, Tara. You managed it really well.

B Thanks very much.

A Did you email the report to the client?

B Oh no! I forgot! I'm really sorry. I'll do it now.

5.5

Joe Joe speaking.

Mandy Hi, Joe. It's Mandy again.

Joe Hi, Mandy.

Mandy I'm sorry, Joe, but we've got a problem with the order for Gosport. We did all the baseball bats and T-shirts yesterday so I can ship them tomorrow. But the logos on the caps didn't work. The colours are wrong. We need to fix the machine today and print them again. I'm really sorry.

Joe OK. Don't worry. I know the Purchasing Manager at Gosport, so I'll speak to him and explain the situation. But can you help me? We need to give another delivery date for this.

Mandy Sure. I'll call the factory now and I'll let you know as soon as I can.

Joe That would be great. Thanks a lot.

5.6

A So what do you think about the use of 'English only' at companies like Honda and Rakuten?

B Well, there are some big advantages. It means that Japanese companies can talk to their customers and suppliers in other countries more easily, as well as to their colleagues who work in offices internationally. They can also save time and money if they don't need to translate documents or have a translator at meetings. And for the employees, they can learn English more easily if they use the language all the time at work.

A And are there any disadvantages?

B Of course. It can be difficult for the company to find good employees who also speak English. And it can be expensive to give them English lessons, and this can take a lot of time, too. Some employees don't want to speak a foreign language at work because they feel they can't say what they want to say in English.

Unit 6

6.1

Martin So, I'm on Twitter and LinkedIn. How can I use social media to get a job?

Georgina Well, the first thing is to have a good profile (on Twitter it's called a 'bio') and a professional profile picture. You need to update your profile regularly and you can also add a link to an online CV.

Martin That's a good idea. And how will companies find my profile?

Georgina Many companies now search online for candidates. But you also have to search for jobs. Many companies are on social media. Look at their pages to find jobs, and you can follow companies on Twitter.

Martin OK, I already do that. What else can I do?

Georgina Well, it's social networking. That means you have to network.

Martin What does that mean I do?

Georgina First, you add contacts to build your network. You can ask your Facebook friends or LinkedIn connections to introduce you to their contacts. You can also search for useful contacts and ask to connect with them. Another good way to find people is to join professional 'groups' on LinkedIn or Facebook. These are called 'communities' on Google+.

Martin I see.

Georgina And it's not enough to have a lot of friends or connections. You have to be active and communicate with your contacts. People need to 'see' you and know something about you. Update your status, that means post something, regularly. Post interesting things that are connected with your work and comment on or 'like' your contacts' posts. Join a group conversation or a Twitter chat, or start a conversation about a professional idea. All of these are easy ways to network.

Martin Thanks very much, Georgina. Useful ideas. I'll go and update my status now.

6.2

Enzo Hello. Can I join you?

Giang Yes, please take a seat. My name's Giang Bai. How do you do?

Enzo My name's Enzo Matti.

Giang Is this your first time in Vietnam?

Enzo Yes, it is. I'm with a textile company in Italy. Here's my card.

Giang Thank you. Here's mine. So you're from Italy. That's a long way to travel. How long did your journey take?

Enzo It took about 48 hours, I think. I came to Ho Chi Minh City last night, but I left Bologna two days ago. I flew to Milan and then to Shanghai. I had a day in Shanghai, so I met some colleagues there yesterday.

Giang Were you on the ten o'clock flight last night?

Enzo That's right.

Giang Oh, we were on the same flight then!

Enzo Really?

6.3

Giang So how did you become a sales manager in textiles?

Enzo Well, my family was always in textiles. My father had his own company in Bologna and I worked for him.

Giang Why did you leave?

Enzo Well, I went to university and I studied Business Management. Then I wanted to work abroad, so I left the family company and spent time in the United States.

Giang So when did you join your current company?

Enzo In 2003.

6.4

A Hi, Mike. How was Brussels?

B Fine, thanks, but the journey was long and tiring.

A Did you go by car?

B Yeah.

A And how was the meeting?

B Very interesting. We discussed a lot of things.

A Was the hotel OK?

B Yes, it was really nice, thanks. Very comfortable, and the food was delicious!

A Sounds good.

6.5

Simon Can I join you?

Nathalie Yes, of course.

Simon I hear you work for GST.

Nathalie Yes, that's right.

Simon My name's Simon Turing. I'm with Tulsa Filters. You're one of our customers.

Nathalie Ah yes. Pleased to meet you. I'm Nathalie Anderson, and this is my colleague, Brent.

Brent Nice to meet you.

Simon And you. So, what do you think of the conference?

Nathalie The conference? Very interesting.

Simon Do you come here every year?

Nathalie No. This is my first time. But Brent here is a regular!

Simon Do you know a lot of people here, Brent?

Brent No, not many. The faces change every year. Would you like another drink?

Simon No, thanks.

Nathalie No, thanks. I'm fine.

Brent Well, please excuse me. I need to go to my room before dinner.

Simon Sure. See you later, maybe.

6.6

A Hello. Can I help you?

B Yes, please. I have an appointment with Mr Cannon, but there's nobody in Reception.

A Oh dear. Is this your first time here?

B Yes, it is.

A Well, come with me. I can take you to his office.

B Thanks very much. After you …

A … OK, right – here's John Cannon's office. Please go in and take a seat.

B Thank you.

A I think John's just next door. I'll call him. Can I get you something? A coffee?

B Oh, yes, please.

A OK, I'll ask him to bring you one. Have a good meeting. Nice talking to you.

B Yes, and you. Bye.

Unit 7

7.1

works	resources
is	departments
organizes	computers
deals	promotes
checks	employees
contacts	services

7.2

Security Good morning, sir.

Jim Hello. I have an appointment at Whitley's.

Security Do you want the factory or the offices?

Jim The offices.

Security Well, you go along this road and turn right. Go past the factory to the offices, but don't park there. Look for the car park sign and drive down below the offices and go into the car park there.

Jim That's great. Thanks a lot.

7.3

1
A This is your visitor's pass.
B Thanks very much.

2
A Those are two of my colleagues.
B Can you introduce me?

3
A These are our new products.
B They look great.

4
A What is that building?
B It's the warehouse.

7.4

1
A Can you spell that?
B Yes, it's Nzogoung. That's N-Z-O-G-O-U-N-G.
A So that's M-Z-O-G-U-N-G.
B No, it's N as in New York, Z, O, G, O as in Oslo, U, N, G.
A Oh, I'm sorry. N-Z-O-G-O-U-N-G.
B That's right.

2
A OK. Can I have a contact number?
B Yes, it's three nine nine, six three four four.
A So, that's three three nine, six three three four. Is that right?
B No, it's three double nine, six three double four.
A Sorry, three nine nine, six three four four.
B Yes.

7.5

A Hello.
B Hello. Could I speak to Teresa Baum, please?
A I'm sorry, but she isn't here this morning. Can I help you?
B Could I leave a message for her?
A Sure.
B It's Richard Andac.
A Can you spell that, please?
B A-N-D-A-C.
A So that's A-N-D-A-C.
B That's right. And I'm calling about our meeting. Can she call me back as soon as possible?
A OK. Can I have a contact number?
B Yes, it's double oh double four, two zero seven, three nine nine, six three four four.
A Sorry, that's double oh double four, two zero seven, three nine nine, six three four four. Is that right?
B Yes.
A OK. I'll give her your message, Mr Andac.
B That's great. Thanks for your help.
A You're welcome.
B Goodbye.

Unit 8

8.1

energetic	practical
imaginative	focused
careful	patient
friendly	experienced

8.2

Anton OK. So we have a student for the summer job. Let's discuss the web editor position next. Who do we have?

Sandra There were lots of emails for this one, but there are only two people really. First of all, there's Monica. I spoke to her on the phone and she's very friendly. At the moment, she works in publishing.

Anton Is she an editor?

Sandra Yes. She has a lot of experience in book editing, but she says she's good at editing websites because she does some in her free time for friends and small businesses.

Anton OK. That sounds like a possibility. What about the other person?

Sandra Here's his picture. Do you recognize him?

Anton Yes, who is he?

Sandra It's Roberto. He was the student on our summer placement last year.

Anton That's right. Roberto! I remember him. Very energetic! Really nice young man.

Sandra Exactly. Anyway, now he has a qualification in IT.

Anton But why is he applying for the web editor job? He doesn't have any experience in editing and he isn't very good at working on his own.

Sandra I know, but he liked it here so much last summer he wants a job. I think he's perfect for the position of web production assistant.

Anton Exactly. Let's offer him that and then invite Monica for an interview. I'd like to see the websites she worked on as well.

Sandra Sure. I'll send you the links.

8.3

1

A Where's Chantelle?

B She isn't working in the office today. She's working at home.

A Why is she doing that?

B She's finishing her report. Her boss wants it for 7.30 tomorrow morning.

2

A Where are Bill and Sofia?

B They're doing the training course for that new finance software.

A Are they doing the course all day?

B No, they aren't. It's only a half-day course.

8.4

1

A Where are you going?

B Home.

A But it's only twelve o'clock.

B I know. But I'm working from home this afternoon.

2

A When are they back from the training course?

B At about 5.45.

3

A She's working on that report today.

B When does her boss want it?

A For 7.30 tomorrow morning.

4

A What time does your train leave?

B At ten past eleven.

8.5

Kasia Hi, Bruno. It's Kasia here.

Bruno Hi, Kasia. How are you?

Kasia Fine, thanks. Listen, we need to meet about the plan for staff to work from home. Can we arrange a meeting on Thursday with Dolores and Chen? Is two o'clock OK for you?

Bruno Sorry, I'm busy then. What about the morning?

Kasia OK. What time are you free?

Bruno 9.30 is good for me.

Kasia I can't meet between 8.00 and 10.00. I've got interviews.

Bruno Are you busy after that?

Kasia Dolores and I have an appointment with someone from the bank at 12.00, so let's meet before that.

Bruno Is 10.15 good for you?

Kasia Yes, a quarter past ten on Thursday is fine. But I don't know about Dolores and Chen. I think Chen has a factory visit in the morning.

Bruno OK. Can you call Dolores and I'll phone Chen?

Kasia Sure.

Bruno Thanks. Bye.

Unit 9

9.1

Interviewer How big is the Accor group?

Manager Well, they employ 190,000 people in nearly a hundred countries. And they have over four thousand hotels worldwide.

Interviewer So, very big.

Manager Yes, but the hotel industry is very competitive – there are a lot of big chains out there.

Interviewer That's true. So, with so many competitors, how does Accor stay competitive?

Manager Well, one reason is that they are the only international group with hotels in every market segment. This means they can offer all their customers a wide choice. For example, Motel 6 is a chain of budget hotels in North America. These offer the customer a cheap option. Then at the economy level there's the All Seasons brand in the Asia-Pacific region. You pay more at these hotels, but they offer very good service with friendly staff.

Interviewer What about hotels for the business traveller who wants more comfort and services?

Manager OK. This is the mid-range market segment. So, we're talking about hotels like Novotel. The quality at a Novotel hotel is very high with modern, up-to-date business facilities like meeting rooms and office services. Location is also important for the customer at these hotels so they are easy to find in city centres or at international airports.

Interviewer And what if money is no problem for the customer?

Manager Then you choose a Sofitel hotel. It's expensive, but it offers five-star quality and each one also offers the visitor something else. Because each country is different, every Sofitel hotel is different and gives the customer a special experience.

9.2

1

A Our competitive advantage is that we provide a better service.

B What do you mean, exactly?

A Well, our staff are more experienced than our competitors' staff. They get six weeks' training before they start.

B So they can give good advice to your customers?

A Yes, that's right. And our staff are friendlier than other shops'. We know our customers well because we often see them.

B What about the products?

A Well, when there's a new product on the market, we're always the first shop in town to stock it. Customers know that our products are more up-to-date. They come here first to see the technology.

2

B What are your competitive advantages?

C Well, the first one is the price. We offer lower prices than our competitors.

B That's because you don't have any shops?

C Yes, but also because we buy products in large quantities. We have 30,000 cubic metres of storage space, so we have bigger stocks than all our competitors.

B Is that an advantage for delivery, too?

C Yes, of course. Because we have large stocks we provide faster delivery. We always deliver in two or three days. And we offer a wider choice – 5,000 different products.

9.3

1

A We have a special low price on this model this month. Only twenty-nine euros ninety-nine.

B That's not bad.

A And then you pay only seventeen euros fifty a month. That's for ten hours of calls.

B Ten hours a month. I don't need ten hours.

A Well, if you prefer five hours a month, it's only eleven seventy-five.

2

A Is delivery free?

B Yes, it is, if you order more than five hundred dollars of goods.

A And if I don't?

B Then there's a delivery charge of seven dollars fifteen cents per item.

A So that's about thirty dollars for four items.

B Yes, twenty-eight sixty to be exact.

3

A That's two thousand, eight hundred and sixty yen, please.

B I have a customer card.

A OK, so that gives you a discount of one hundred and seventy yen today. So that's two thousand, six hundred and ninety yen.

9.4

Managing Director So, did you look at the two quotes for the website?

Javier Yes, briefly. Here they are.

Managing Director OK. How do they compare?

Javier For price, ITE is cheaper.

Managing Director Yes, so I see. Why is that?

Javier They're a smaller, newer company. It's two brothers. Weblines is older and it has about 20 staff.

Managing Director Are they better?

Javier The quality is similar. Weblines produces very nice sites, but ITE also does good work. The advantage of ITE is the two people have experience in the online marketing and sales industry. The disadvantage of Weblines is they don't usually work with online businesses.

Managing Director How fast can they do the work?

Javier There's no difference. They both need four months.

Managing Director Four?

Javier That's fairly normal.

Managing Director I see. Well, what do you think?

Javier I prefer ITE. They're cheaper, they're professional, but also easy to talk to. I like their work – it's more modern.

Managing Director Fine. Let's choose them.

Javier Good. I'll call them today.

9.5

A So, these two German supermarkets are doing very well in Britain. Why is that? Is it all about price?

B Of course, price is very important. They are called discount supermarkets, because they offer low prices, but quality is important, too. The German customers expect good quality at low prices and that's what the British customers want, too.

A And how can they offer such low prices?

B Firstly, they have a much smaller range of products than the bigger supermarkets, like Tesco or Sainsbury's: an average of 1,350 in a UK Aldi, compared with 25,000 products in a UK Tesco. And they don't sell many famous name brands. This means that they get cheaper prices from the suppliers and they can have smaller stores.

A But don't customers want a wider choice of products?

B A lot of customers like the smaller stores because it's faster and easier to do their shopping.

A It's interesting that both companies are German. Is there something especially German that makes them successful?

B Well, they do have very good systems that save time and money. For example, all deliveries are to a central distribution centre so that they can control deliveries to the stores. And these systems are the same in all their stores in different countries. Did you know that Aldi operates in 17 different countries and Lidl in 31? The idea of good quality at a low price is also the same in all these countries. But Aldi and Lidl do make some changes for the local market. For example, Aldi offers online shopping in Australia but not in Europe, and in all countries they also sell food which is produced locally. In the UK, they have successful TV advertisements – something they don't do in Germany. Lidl is also using social media very successfully and is now the European food retailer brand with the most 'likes' on Facebook!

A Really? Very interesting. Thanks very much, Dominic.

Unit 10

10.1

Zoe Is everything OK, Rashid?

Rashid Well, I have a big problem with the new project team.

Zoe Oh! What's the matter?

Rashid They're nice people and they're working hard, but there's a serious problem with their teamwork. They're just not working together. They don't share information with each other or try to find solutions to problems together. So it means that sometimes two people do the same task, or they waste a lot of time trying to find information, instead of asking someone on the team.

Zoe I see. That's a difficult problem. Do they know each other?

Rashid Yes. We had a meeting at the beginning of the project where we introduced everybody and everybody could talk to each other.

Zoe Maybe it wasn't enough. Can you do some kind of team-building? Take everyone out for lunch together or go to a café after work? Give them time to get to know each other better.

Rashid That's a nice idea!

Zoe And why don't you have a team meeting every morning? Everyone could share information and ask each other questions.

Rashid That might not be a bad solution, but a daily meeting takes up a lot of time.

Zoe Or how about talking to them all about their teamwork?

Rashid I don't think that's such a good idea. I don't want them to think I'm telling them what to do. It's difficult to decide. I'll think about it.

10.2

Richard Hello.

Adriana Hi, Richard. It's Adriana.

Richard How are things in Recife?

Adriana Not good, I'm afraid. The problem is bigger than we thought.

Richard Oh no! Not because of the new components? They were so expensive!

Adriana No, I know they were the most expensive solution, but they were also the best idea.

Richard So what's the real problem?

Adriana Well, Pedro says the new components are worse than the old components, but the team leaders say they are better, and I agree.

Richard So are you saying the problem isn't technical?

Adriana That's right. I think it's a personnel problem. Do you know that staff turnover in Recife is the highest? Our other factories are about 30% lower.

Richard Wow. That is surprising. So the problem is the team?

Adriana No, not the team. It's the Line Manager. The biggest problem is Pedro. No one likes him.

10.3

1
A I got a promotion to Section Manager.
B Great. That's fantastic!

2
A I didn't get that sales job that I applied for.
B I'm sorry. How disappointing.

3
A I left my phone on the train.
B Oh no. That's terrible.

4
A Our boss got a new job with our biggest competitor.
B Wow. That is surprising.

5
A Our company won retailer of the year.
B Really? How amazing!

6
A We won the contract for the new shopping centre.
B Good. That's excellent news!

10.4

Director So. Did you read the report?

Line Manager Yes.

Director And? What's your opinion?

Line Manager I think it explains some of the problems, but not all. For example, we have the highest prices, so in my opinion that's one reason. But some customers also say that our delivery times are slow.

Director I agree. And it isn't just delivery that's slow. Look at the figures for the call centre. We have the longest call times. Do you think they need more training?

Line Manager I don't think so. All the staff get regular training. Maybe it's a problem of teamwork. I think we should make them feel part of a team where people like working.

Director I'm not so sure.

Unit 11

11.1

A Hello. Clarion Hotel.

B Hello. I'm calling from Dublin airport. I've missed my flight, so I'd like to book a room for the night. Do you have any vacancies?

A Yes, we have a double room at one hundred and twenty euros.

B Does that include breakfast?

A Yes, it does.

B Great. Can I book a room then?

A Certainly. Can I have your name?

B It's Ms Chiang. C-H-I-A-N-G.

A And I need your credit card details.

B Sure. It's Visa.

A And what's the card number?

B 6674 8596 8374 6374.

A And what's the expiry date?

B Zero three, nineteen.

A OK, Ms Chiang. That's a double room for just one night. You can check in anytime now.

B Sorry, where is the hotel exactly?

A We're on the airport grounds. There's a free bus from the terminal.

B Thanks very much. See you later.

11.2

A Good evening, madam.

B Hello. My name is Chiang. I have a reservation for tonight.

A That's right. Can I see your credit card, please?

B Here you are.
A Thank you. Your room is on the fifth floor. Room five-oh-one. The lift is over there.
B Thanks. What time is breakfast served?
A It's between five and ten a.m. There's also dinner in the hotel restaurant this evening until ten.
B Do I need to book a table?
A No, you don't.

11.3

A Hello. Reception.
B Hello. This is Ms Chiang in room five-oh-one. Can I have a wake-up call, please?
A Certainly. What time is that for?
B Six a.m., please. Also, can you order me a taxi to the airport terminal for seven o'clock?
A Yes, we can arrange that.
B Sorry, there's one other thing. Do the rooms have Internet access? I can't log on.
A Yes, they do, but there's a problem with the connection this evening. Sorry, we're trying to fix it now.
B OK. I'd also like dinner in my room. Do you have room service?
A Yes, one moment, please …

11.4

A When is your trip to Canada?
B Next week.
A Why are you going?
B To visit the sales offices. I'm going to visit Toronto first to see the sales reps there.
A Great. Are you going to Vancouver as well?
B No, I'm not going to have time. But I'm going to spend a day in Quebec to present the new product to Dominic and his team.
A Oh! Quebec is beautiful.
B Yes, I think we're going out in the evening to see the old city and have dinner.
A When are you coming back?
B On Thursday, but I'm going to take Friday off to have a nice long weekend.
A Good idea!

11.5

1
A Here you are. The terminal is there.
B Thanks. How much is that?
A Eighteen pounds, please.
B Here's twenty. Keep the change. Can I have a receipt?
A Sure.

2
A Can I help you?
B I'd like something for my children. How much do these cost?
A They're twenty-nine euros each.
B OK. I need two. Can I pay by credit card?
A Sure.

3
A Hello. Can I help you?
B I'd like to change five hundred dollars into euros, please.
A Certainly. The exchange rate is one point two three today. Is that OK?
B What's the total?
A Four hundred and six euros.
B OK.
A Do you want the notes in fifties?
B Yes, that's fine.
A So that's four hundred and six euros and your receipt.
B Thanks very much.

11.6

A I think we've just got time for lunch before we fly.
B Good. I'm hungry!
A OK, there's a nice Italian place just over there.
B Sounds good!
…
A Do you like pizza? They have really good pizza here.
B Yes, I do, but I think the risotto looks nice.
C Hello. Are you ready to order?
A Yes, please. We'd like a bottle of sparkling water and … would you like to order first?
B OK. I'll have the vegetable risotto, please.
C OK.
A And I'd like the pepperoni pizza, please.
C Sure, so one vegetable risotto and one pepperoni pizza. Would you like any side dishes?
B Not for me, thanks.
A No, thanks.
…
B How was your meal?
A Very nice. And yours?
B Delicious! Would you like a dessert?
A No, thanks. I'll just have a coffee.
B Me, too. Excuse me?
C Yes?
B We'd like two coffees, please.
C Sure.
B And could I have the bill, please?
C Of course. Just a moment.

Unit 12

12.1

1
Sixty per cent of all major international trade fairs now take place in my country and January to mid-May is the really busy period. So I can usually take my annual leave in June or July and then some more time off in the autumn before I start planning again for next year.

2
I have a very busy schedule at the start and end of the year. In January, we have the sales, with big discounts, so lots of customers like to shop then. And, of course, through November and December we have the build-up to Christmas, so that's our busiest time. The summer is a quiet period because people go on holiday and spend more time outside and less time in shops. September gets busier as people do 'back to school' shopping.

3
We promise to deliver flowers the same day so we have very tight deadlines. We also need to be sure we have the right number of staff. For certain public holidays or special occasions, like Valentine's Day and Mother's Day, we need about 80 people and five team leaders. Spring is definitely our busiest time of year. During quiet weeks we only have about ten full-time staff in the centre.

12.2

Greta Hello. Greta Helsing speaking.
Barati Hi, Greta. It's Barati in Kathmandu.
Greta Oh, hi, Barati.
Barati Hi. Thanks for your email about the Palmarosa oil. We've sent it and it's going to arrive on the twenty-seventh. I know you have a tight deadline, but we've had a few problems here.
Greta Don't worry. The twenty-seventh is OK. I can change the schedule by a week.
Barati Have you taken lots of orders for the soap?
Greta Yes, there's been a lot of interest.
Barati Great. Have you seen some of the other products on our website?
Greta Yes, I have. They look really interesting.
Barati You should come and visit us sometime. Have you ever been to Nepal?
Greta No, I haven't, but I'd love to!

12.3

1
A So, what are the busy times for you?
B People usually think about buying and selling houses in spring, so my busiest period is in spring.
A And are you busy now?
B Well, I'm travelling to a big real estate conference tomorrow. My flight is at ten. The conference starts on the thirteenth, but I've got some meetings first. So, yes, I'm quite busy.

2
A What are you going to do at the weekend?
B Working! I always work at weekends as that's our busiest time – and holidays. We are open on public holidays.
A When can you take time off?
B I have a day off in the week and the restaurant is closed in May, so I have my annual leave then.

12.4

Greta At the moment, the schedule is about a week late. The situation is that the raw material from Nepal has just arrived and we've already taken it to the warehouse. So the aim is to get the soap on the shelves by Valentine's Day.
Soledad But what's the deadline for this? I know we need it for February the fourteenth, but what date is the launch?
Greta We plan to launch it on January the twentieth.
Soledad But Martin, how much time do we need for production?
Martin Production isn't a problem. But we haven't got a final package yet.
Greta I know. I've spoken to the designers again today. We'll have the packaging by the thirty-first of October.
Martin OK. So we'll have the final product by the end of December?
Greta That's right. Around the twentieth.
Soledad Why don't we deliver the product at the beginning of January? The shops are going to want it earlier than the twentieth.
Greta OK. Then let's start delivery from the warehouse on January the second. Is everyone happy with that date?
Martin/Soledad Fine./No problem.
Greta Right. So, to summarize, I'm going to call our packaging people – again. And we're going to tell clients they'll have the product by January the …?
Soledad Let's say January the fifth. I'll tell them. And I'm going to prepare some press releases as well.
Greta Great.

Irregular verb list

Verb	Past simple	Past participle	Verb	Past simple	Past participle
be	was/were	been	let	let	let
become	became	become	light	lit	lit
begin	began	begun	lose	lost	lost
break	broke	broken	make	made	made
bring	brought	brought	mean	meant	meant
build	built	built	meet	met	met
burn	burnt/burned	burnt/burned	pay	paid	paid
buy	bought	bought	put	put	put
catch	caught	caught	read	read	read
choose	chose	chosen	ride	rode	ridden
come	came	come	ring	rang	rung
cost	cost	cost	rise	rose	risen
cut	cut	cut	run	ran	run
deal	dealt	dealt	say	said	said
do	did	done	see	saw	seen
dream	dreamt	dreamt	sell	sold	sold
drink	drank	drunk	send	sent	sent
drive	drove	driven	set	set	set
eat	ate	eaten	shine	shone	shone
fall	fell	fallen	show	showed	shown
feed	fed	fed	shut	shut	shut
feel	felt	felt	sing	sang	sung
fight	fought	fought	sit	sat	sat
find	found	found	sleep	slept	slept
fly	flew	flown	speak	spoke	spoken
forget	forgot	forgotten	spell	spelt/spelled	spelt/spelled
freeze	froze	frozen	spend	spent	spent
get	got	got	stand	stood	stood
give	gave	given	steal	stole	stolen
go	went	gone/been	swim	swam	swum
grow	grew	grown	take	took	taken
have	had	had	teach	taught	taught
hear	heard	heard	tell	told	told
hide	hid	hidden	think	thought	thought
hold	held	held	throw	threw	thrown
keep	kept	kept	understand	understood	understood
know	knew	known	wake	woke	woken
lead	led	led	wear	wore	worn
learn	learnt/learned	learnt/learned	win	won	won
leave	left	left	write	wrote	written
lend	lent	lent			

OXFORD
UNIVERSITY PRESS

Great Clarendon Street, Oxford, OX2 6DP, United Kingdom

Oxford University Press is a department of the University of Oxford.
It furthers the University's objective of excellence in research, scholarship,
and education by publishing worldwide. Oxford is a registered trade
mark of Oxford University Press in the UK and in certain other countries

ISBN: 978 0 19 473870 5   (book)
ISBN: 978 0 19 473866 8   (pack)

Printed in China

This book is printed on paper from certified and well-managed sources

ACKNOWLEDGEMENTS

*The authors and publisher are grateful to those who have given permission to reproduce
the following extracts and adaptations of copyright material*: p.71 Adapted extract
from "Kaiser Permanente Uses the Myers-Briggs® Assessment to Enhance a
Broad Range of Training" and quick fact from www.cpp.com. Reproduced with
permission from the publisher, CPP, Inc. Copyright 2016. All rights reserved.
Further reproduction is prohibited without CPP's written consent. For more
information, please visit www.cpp.com.

Sources: p.08 www.marcegaglia.com p.13 www.kikkoman.com p.14
http://english.cj.net p.18 www.lego.com p.32 www.orsgroup.com
p.32 www.link2portal.com p.51 www.designbuild-network.com p.58
www.accor.com p.66 www.fastcompany.com p.74 www.cityrunningtours.com

*The publisher would like to thank the following for their permission to reproduce
photographs*: Alamy pp.12 (4/Roger Bamber, 8/seewhatmitchsee), 14 (A/MIXA),
31 (E/WorkImages), 32 (flags/YAY Media AS), 36 (Bert Hoferichter), 37 (Uniqlo/
age footstock), 40 (Hero Images Inc.), 42 (rooftop/Hero Images Inc., reception/
Cultura RM), 53 (A/Blend Images), 53 (C/Dorset Media Service), 56 (Image
Source), 58 (Sofitel/BSTAR IMAGES), 63 (supermarket signs/dpa picture alliance
archive), 71 (Bill Cheyrou), 78 (florist/Vadym Drobot, trade show/FocusEurope,
department store/eye35.pix), 84 (restaurant/caia image), 110 (2/Wavebreak
Media Ltd), 112 (airport/Crispin Rodwell, meeting/Big Cheese Photo
LLC), 115 (2/Wavebreak Media Ltd), 119 (hotel room/Dirk v. Mallinckrodt,
sandwiches/Murad RM); Getty pp.6 (all), 10, 11, 12 (train station/Dong Wenjie),
13 (C/Ian O'Leary), 14 (B), 18 (3/Alberto Incrocci), 24 (View Pictures), 26 (fibre
optics), 26 (6), 30, 32 (pile of paper), 34, 37 (Honda/Bloomberg), 38 (motorway),
46 (pigeon holes/John Humble, c, f/VisitBritain/Chris Renton), 51 (View
Pictures), 52, 54 (Sean De Burca), 57, 58 (cyclists), 62 (Kelvin Murray), 66 (shop/
Bloomberg), 68 (Pedro), 72 (taxis), 74 (Andrew Watson), 76 (Thomas Barwick),
77, 78 (departures board), 84 (reception/John Warburton-Lee), 110 (3),
112 (hotel/Tim Graham, dessert, Paris/Jon Hicks), 115 (3), 119 (airport/Peter
Adams, meeting/Regina Casagrande); Oxford University Press pp.9, 13 (D),
17 (wheat field, Budapest), 18 (1), 26 (5), 31 (A), 46 (g), 53 (D, E), 60 (shop),
63 (trolleys), 72 (receptionist), 85; Rex Features pp.14 (C/Seong Joon Cho);
Shutterstock pp.8, 12 (1, 2, 3, 5, 6, 7), 13 (A, B), 14 (D), 17 (flag, sunflowers,
oil rig, fabric), 18 (map, 2, 4, 5, Lego® men), 20, 23 (all), 26 (mobile banking
on phone, 1–4), 31 (circuit board), 31 (B–D, F), 38 (people using tech), 43, 44,
46 (a, b, d, e, h), 50, 53 (B, F), 58 (hotel reception), 60 (girl), 64, 66, 68 (Richard,
Adriana), 80, 82, 83, 84 (departures board), 110 (1), 115 (1), 119 (Chicago).

With special thanks to: Kiva Systems p.28

Illustrations by: Mark Duffin pp.27, 33; Becky Halls/The Organisation p.75;
Martin Sanders pp.6, 49, 99, 113, 119.

Cover image: Getty Images/Clerkenwell

Back cover photograph: Oxford University Press building/David Fisher

*The authors and publisher would also like to thank the following individuals for their
advice and assistance in developing the material for this course*: Beth Alexander,
Angelica Anastacio Molzahn, Clare Burke, Linda Cox, Louise Dixon, Simon
Drury, Justin Ehresman, Tom Evans, Jane Hoatson, Annie Kavaka, Christen
Kisch, Catherine Mayer, Sean O'Malley, Graeme Romanes, Rachael Smith,
Greg Steven, Edward Taylor.

*Although every effort has been made to trace and contact copyright holders before
publication, this has not been possible in some cases. We apologize for any apparent
infringement of copyright and if notified, the publisher will be pleased to rectify any
errors or omissions at the earliest opportunity.*